NOWHERE TO RUN

Val Yare's True Story
with Nick Towle

Nick Towle ©
Facebook.com/Warcrypress

ISBN: 978-1-912543-20-5

NOWHERE TO RUN - Val Yare's True Story

NOWHERE TO RUN - Val Yare's True Story produced by www.wacrypress.co.uk (part of Roobix Ltd: 7491233) on behalf of Nick Towle, Snaith. Copyright © Nick Towle 2018 has asserted his right as the author of this work in accordance with the Copyright, Designs and Patents Act 1988.

Printed and bound in Great Britain by Carter & Jackson, Pontefract.

Find out more at: facebook.com/warcrypress

'On the last and greatest day of the festival, Jesus stood and said in a loud voice, "Let anyone who is thirsty come to me and drink. Whoever believes in me, as Scripture has said, rivers of living water will flow from within them".'

John 7:37-38

Contents

Acknowledgements

Writing this book has been a painful journey for me in many ways. It has brought back some unpleasant memories that I would rather have forgotten.

However, looking back at all the ups and downs in my life, I realise that all that has happened has made me the person I am today, and I no longer take people at face-value, as the reader will understand.

I would like to thank those who have been with me on this journey. Firstly, to Nick Towle, who has helped me pen this story and been a model of patience and rigour. And to my husband Bill for his love and support, and especially for his proof-reading skills.

To my daughter Victoria, for jogging my memory over dates that I had forgotten, and for encouraging me to write this book.

Last but by no means least, to my lovely neighbour Sandra, who unwittingly came up with the name for this book. One day, when I was briefly telling her my story, she said: "Oh, you were so young and you had nowhere to run." It was a eureka moment and I said: "That's it, that's what I will name the book."

Val Yare

Editor's Acknowledgements

A big thanks to everyone involved in the production of this book, especially Mrs Val Yare, a remarkable lady in many ways who has been dealt so many harsh blows in her life but had the guts and tenacity to come back fighting.

It's been a privilege to get to know Val and an absolute pleasure to work with her on this intriguing project, which has been ten months in the making. I have to say I've enjoyed every single minute, notwithstanding her steadfast attention to detail!

Thanks also to Bill Yare, her husband of 50 years and a wonderful fellow who, along with his devoted wife, welcomed me into his home and showed me such warm hospitality.

A big thanks also to Rob Brenton of Warcry Press, Jubilee Church and of course my family, not least my father Dennis Towle for showing me the ropes and encouraging me to scribble down words for a living.

Finally, a kind of warped thanks to all the cads, rogues and bounders who have invested this story with all the bone-chilling malevolence and double-dealing that throws into sharp relief the strength and stoicism of our eponymous heroine.

Nick Towle

Foreword

There was just something about this man that drew me to him. I don't know what it was exactly: he wasn't particularly handsome, but he had a quiet dignity which I found appealing.

He dressed neatly but not flamboyantly; he was tall and kept himself to himself. He wasn't loud and brash like the other Americans and had the bearing of a man who was comfortable in his own flesh. He was lean, willowy, with a good head of dark-brown hair, but he was certainly no George Clooney.

While the other Americans drank and caroused and chased the local girls, he sloped off quietly to his hotel room. I imagined him as the thoughtful, caring type, one who knew his path in life but never had to raise his voice.

I was wrong on all counts - hopelessly so - but I only realised I'd made the mistake of my life after I married the guy. I didn't realise how strange our coming together must have seemed to those around me: the petite, bespectacled little northern girl and this ever-so-quiet American who never drank, never chased the ladies and never uttered a cross word.

Looking back, it was an odd arrangement from the word go, but I never gave it a moment's thought. I was blinded by love and never saw the man behind the mask until it was too late. I failed to see beyond the façade and paid the heaviest price. I was naïve in the extreme; hoodwinked by a consummate fraudster. And I'd staked my life on him.

I was a starry-eyed young woman with every advantage in life when I fell for this impostor, but the consequences of my fateful error echo to this day.

I'm older and wiser now, but I still wonder how on earth I managed to get caught up in his web of lies and deceit. It's a conundrum with no answers. I still wonder at how he thought he could get away with it. He must have been very convincing to a 20-year-old girl with dreams of marriage.

The painful and bitter experience has made me a much harder person than I used to be. I no longer take people at face value and I have no time for liars.

Writing this book has itself been a painful journey. It has brought back some unpleasant memories that I would rather forget.

But looking back at all the horrors and ups and downs in my life, I realise that all that has happened to me has made me the person I am today.

Human beings are the most complex of creatures. Spite and meanness are in our DNA, and I discovered to my cost that your worst enemies can be those you trust the most.

I have borne this cross for 50 years or more and I want this to be a lesson to you all: wolves come in sheep's clothing. People are not what they are; crooks and conmen lurk around every corner. I just hope that you don't have the misfortune to meet one as I did.

If nothing else, I sincerely hope that for those who read on, my own naivety serves as a warning to all those young women out there who think they've found 'Mr Right' but may well be dancing with the devil.

I tell you my story not for sympathy, nor for vindication or revenge. I just tell it like it is and let you decide whether I was duped through my own simplicity, or simply paid the price for falling madly in love with a man I thought I knew, but never really knew at all.

Everything I tell you is the unvarnished truth. There's no need for tinsels and bells: I lived through a nightmare that requires no exaggeration...

Chapter 1

Her Hands

Mother was a cruel woman. She never showed me an ounce of affection and it's clear to me now that I was an unwanted baby.

To be raised in such circumstances is an unusual and thankfully rare occurrence, but then mother was an unusual and rare woman.

From taking my first steps out of the cot to earning top marks at school, I never felt loved or wanted by her.

Such a hard woman, and she hit me as a matter of course. It was obvious she never really wanted me, yet I yearned for motherly attention and would do anything to please her. Nothing ever did.

My father was a different kettle of fish. I put him on a pedestal and for the first three decades of my life, he was - in my eyes at least - a saint without question. I was, in many ways, a daddy's girl, but, oh, how little I knew.

There are people out there you will have lived among, worked with, known for years, and you think you know them. They live this lie for 30 years or more, then one day the whole façade comes tumbling down and you realise the person you thought you knew only existed in your imagination. It's a hoax that can last a lifetime and only after you discover the fraud do you realise how thin the veil really was.

I was born Hazel Valerie Jackson near the end of the war, at my nana's house in Grove Hill, Middlesbrough. It was 9.50pm and Housewives' Choice was on the radio. I think I must have been conceived during my parents' honeymoon. They dropped my first name and I became Valerie, or 'Our Valerie' to my relations.

Five years before I was born, Middlesbrough was blitzed by the Luftwaffe. It was the first British town to be bombed by the Germans because of its heavy industries: steel, shipping, the chemical plants, which are now almost extinct.

On the first day of the raids, a German plane dropped 13 bombs on a huge chunk of land between South Bank Road and the South Steel Plant. One of the bombs fell on the South Bank football ground and a huge crater destroyed half the pitch.

The railway station got hit too: one of the bombs shattered the old Victorian glass and another caved in part of the steel roof. A train was badly damaged, though mercifully there were no passengers inside.

My mother, a young girl at the time, was at the station when it got hit. She was with her Aunty Louis and Uncle Ray who were waving someone off. When the bomb struck, Uncle Ray laid on top of his pregnant wife to protect her from flying shrapnel. The only bit of her that he didn't cover was her arm, which was badly injured. She was scarred for life.

My maternal grandparents lived in the same road as Brian Clough's childhood home. My father's parents lived just around the corner in a fire-station house.

My paternal grandfather, Bob Jackson senior, was a fireman, and that sort of living arrangement wasn't uncommon in those days.

One day, a German bomber dropped its load on Albert Park, just opposite the fire station, during a period of heavy bombardment. By the end of the blitz, we'd lost over 200 buildings, mainly factories, industrial plants and Victorian terraced houses.

They tried to patch the place up, but, to be honest, the town has never looked the same since. We took quite a hit and even Churchill came over to boost morale and inspect our coastal defences.

I grew up in a town which, to all intents and purposes, was on the slide, but I was cosseted in many ways by the trappings of a middle-class family in one of the newest parts of Middlesbrough. I didn't really want for anything and my father ran his own business, so money was never an issue. Compared to others, we were posh, I suppose, though I never really gave it a second thought because that's the way it had always been.

Dad treated me kindly in the main, but, oh, he was strict, though he never laid a finger on me. And then there was mother and her hands.

She knew how to slap alright. She left marks and from the age of five, not a week went by without me feeling the back of her hand. I understand she had a very bad time giving birth to me and that there was no bond when I came out of the womb. She swore there and then that she wouldn't have another child. She didn't.

Once, when I was about seven or eight, she pushed me so hard against the gas oven the knobs stuck in my back. I was sobbing my eyes out. It hurt like hell.

She only really stopped hitting me when I got to secondary school. I really don't remember what brought the attacks on, if anything at all. I just remember her losing her temper and going red in the face, her eyes bulging out. I wet the bed for years, until I was about nine or 10, mainly because of the attacks, but also because I was so frightened of them both. You didn't dare step out of line, ever. It was almost always mother, and I didn't dare say anything to her either during or after the attacks.

Once, we were having Sunday lunch and she put cabbage on my plate. I hated cabbage and told her I didn't want any. She played holy hell and made me eat it. I did as I was told, then threw up all over the dinner table. She was so shocked she never gave me cabbage again - not because I didn't like cabbage, but because she was scared to death that if she forced me to eat it, she might have to clean up her precious dining table again. The funny thing is, I love cabbage now.

I grew up an only child but in no way a loved one as far as mother was concerned. I never felt wanted by her and she gave me no reason to believe that she felt an ounce of compassion towards me. She was a pitiless woman, hard to the core and didn't show me one iota of affection. To be perfectly honest, she didn't know how to show affection.

When my father showed me love, it would drive her mad with jealousy. He was on leave from the RAF when he married her at The Avenue Methodist Church in 1944. It was a double wedding: his sister, Lena, got married in the same church on the same day.

Father was no dashing airline pilot. He was based in Palestine and then neutral Reykjavik, the Icelandic capital, during the war. The British got a foothold in Iceland in 1941 - apparently illegally - to prevent any German incursions from Denmark, which the Nazis had taken a year earlier, and to prevent shipments reaching

7

Germany from the Icelandic ports. Father was probably there as an engineer or something, but I never asked.

My first few months were spent at my nana's house when the war was nearing its end and the town recovered from the barrage. My parents, Bob and Vi (short for Violet), were still living on their wits and had always lived with my mother's parents until they could find a council house of their own. But council houses were in short supply, partly due to the air raids but mainly because everyone was waiting for the authorities to build the new estates, so when we moved out of my nana's we lived on an old army camp, which had been decommissioned after the war.

There were at least 20 families on the army base, living in spartan accommodation which was basic to the core. It was like a commune for the dispossessed because many people had got married during the war and had lots of children, but they had nowhere to house them because they hadn't built enough council homes.

Middlesbrough paid a heavy price for the post-war baby boom and most of the people on the camp were young couples with kids, living out of a suitcase 'cos they had nowhere else to go. Because of the bombings, heavy industry had to be relocated to the outskirts of the town and the original Middlesbrough, which was 'over the border', past the train station, was left to languish. In the old days, houses were built inside the steelworks and the industrial plants, and kids used to take their dads' dinners while they were at work.

We spent 18 months on the army base, living in the sergeants' mess on what is now the Beechwood Estate. The sergeants' mess was the biggest building on the camp, so we were privileged, I suppose. Heaven knows why we got the mess because there were only three of us and there were much bigger families on the site. The building was made of corrugated steel and had a rounded roof. It used to shake when a fair wind got up.

We had a kitchen and a lounge with a dining room and at least two bedrooms. It was very long and spacious, and we didn't even have neighbours because the place was blocked off where our living quarters ended, but it was freezing in winter and we didn't have a bathroom as such, just a toilet and sink. We had one bath a week in an old tub in front of a coal fire in the main room.

There was this one family on the camp who frightened the life out of me because I'd overheard my mother telling my father that the husband used to beat his wife. Occasionally, mother would send me over to this family's house on errands and I absolutely dreaded it because I was terrified of the man who beat up his wife. I told mother I was frightened, but she sent me anyway.

I didn't like it on the camp. The only thing I looked forward to were our regular visits to my nana's, which were a blessed relief. Mother used to cycle there with me on the back seat of her bike. Nana would welcome us with tea from the pot and a plate of chocolate biscuits.

We finally got ourselves a brand-new council house in the Thorntree estate when I was three. Mother was made up because it had an inside toilet and a bathroom - still a luxury back then. She was floating on air for the first few months but her good mood didn't last long. She still hit me and shunned me at every turn. Not maternal in any way.

Thorntree was a lovely place to live in those days, like so many proud working-class communities. Nowadays it's full of druggies and the long-term unemployed. A lot of the estates have gone that way, but we loved it because it was a different world back then.

My father was working for ICI, the big chemical firm, as an instrument artificer, then set up his own business repairing domestic appliances like washing machines and Hoovers. He set up a shop in town and earned enough money to employ some guys in the workshop. They looked up to him, but he was a hard taskmaster.

He was a very popular guy and the business was booming, so he paid them a fair wage. He drove flashy cars like a gold Vauxhall Velox and he liked big motors. Maybe it was because he was such a small man – he only stood at 5ft 6.

I remember a boy at my junior school used to look at me in awe and said: "Your dad's got a Vauxhall Velox!"

"Oh, yeah," I said, and just shrugged, as if it was nothing out of the ordinary. But this boy was amazed.

"He's the only man on this estate with a car like that!" he said, as if he'd just witnessed the Eighth Wonder of the World.

9

I have to say, it meant nothing to me and I couldn't understand what he was getting so worked up about. To me, it was just the norm, but to this boy the Velox was a modern wonder.

Father was indeed the first one on our estate to have a big, flashy car; what they called a "posh" car. We became what I suppose you would call well-off. I never wanted for anything and was kitted out in nice clothes. The people we knew were all relatively well-off and the money we had squirrelled away meant we were shielded from the poverty that had gripped the town in the post-war years.

In keeping with a comfortable middle-class upbringing, I buried my head in books and became quite a studious child. I read the works of the Bronte sisters avidly. I was obsessed with Jane Eyre and Wuthering Heights, which are still my favourite books.

I would catch the bus from Thorntree to the library in North Ormesby two miles away and just lose myself in the bleak moorlands of Howarth. For some reason I got into the habit of buying books about ballet dancers. I don't know why, because I was never into ballet and never wanted to be a ballerina. Strange, that.

I was top in every class at Caldicotes Junior School. I was very clever, the star pupil. I never misbehaved, never got into any trouble and I was a bit of a teachers' pet, if truth be told. I loved learning and it all came so easily to me. I got top grades in all the subjects - reading and writing especially, because I loved languages. I was a very creative child, perhaps because I'm left-handed.

In those days, if you did wrong you went to the front of the class and the teacher, Mr Blake, would get his deck shoes out – what we called 'sand shoes'. He was a big size 8.

You had to bend over and he would either hit you on the bum with the sand shoe or strike you on the back of the hand. I was a good girl: I only remember him hitting me once.

Mr Blake was strict. I had him in my last two years at junior school and you daren't stray out of line. You didn't talk back to teachers back then; you did as you were told. And woe betide anyone who misbehaved.

I look back at those school photos now and it's like a different world: there's me at the end of the row, with my round glasses and unruly hair; and there's Mr Blake, looking like one of those austere Victorian schoolmasters, with the whole form practically cowering under his steely gaze.

After school we played out in the street: in truth, we were never in. There were no cars and the streets were your oyster, your playground. You learned so much when you played outside. We were adventurous, we were game, and we made things up. We played skips and 'two-ball', where you played the ball up against a wall. 'Two-ball' because you played with two balls.

I remember once we walked up to Eston Hills three miles away with a bottle of water and some sandwiches. I remember it seemed quite glamorous at the time because the nearby township was Eston, California, and for us it was like being up in the Hollywood hills. They mine ironstone up there.

I was an outdoor child but I hated sports: I just couldn't get my head around them. I wasn't co-ordinated that way.

In the Girl Guides, I was centre stage. By the age of 11, I was a patrol leader in the Fuchsia Patrol. I enjoyed leadership from an early age and was quite a natural in the role. You had to go to church if you were in the Guides and the highlight of our year was carrying the standards down the aisle during the annual procession. I used to lead the troop, holding the Fuchsia banner aloft at the head of the line at St Thomas's on The Brambles Farm estate. On one occasion, I held the banner a little too high and it swept the church lights, knocking them flat one by one. The clergy were none too impressed.

I was very popular with the other children, but when all the other kids went home to mother and tea, there was no-one home at our house. I always had to let myself in from school because dad would be busy in the workshop and mum worked at the butcher's on the estate. I felt so lonely and scared in that house alone.

One day there was a knock at the door - I was petrified. I opened the door and standing there was this Indian guy in a long, flowery dress. He was trying to sell something; I can't remember what. I was shaking with fright because I'd never seen an Indian man in Middlesbrough before. I shut the door on him and ran into my room, hiding under the covers. The poor man was probably a lovely chap just trying to earn a living, but I was alone and absolutely terrified.

Another time, I came home from school and went to the outside toilet out back where my mother kept the old mangle that she used on washing days and left the key to the front door. I creaked the door open and went in to get the key, only to find an unsuspecting paperboy having a wee. I screamed blue murder, a blood-curdling scream that brought the man next-door running out of his house. There was an older man who was out the back, shovelling coal in the next yard.

"Are you alright?" he yelled.

And then the paperboy comes running out, shouting: "I'm so sorry!"

We were, to all intents and purposes, a normal family, though I would discover years later that this was a misnomer. We went to the pictures and enjoyed holidays and picnics, but I was always at my grandparents' in the school holidays because my mother was busy at work. My grandparents were lovely, not at all like my mother.

My granddad, Harry Stanton, was a well-known comedian in Middlesbrough and performed all over the North East. His stage name was 'Geordie' Stanton, though he was a Teessider, not a Geordie. People said he was like Bobby Thompson, the famous stand-up comedian and actor from Newcastle, so that's why my granddad got the nickname 'Geordie'. He had a great turn of phrase and even though I was a little girl I still got his dry sense of humour.

During the bombardments, my nana and granddad kept an Anderson shelter in the back yard. When there was an air-raid on, my granddad would drop his newspaper, stub out his cigarette and head straight for the shelter. My nana, Winnie, would be looking high and low for her dentures in a state of utter panic.

"Hang on," she'd say. "I haven't got any teeth!"

My granddad, God bless him, would turn around and look at her as if she'd lost her marbles.

"They're dropping bombs," he'd say, "not bloody sandwiches!"

Chapter 2

Thieves Don't Leave Notes

I was overjoyed when father bought a spaniel pup for the home on the camp, but the poor thing spent most of his time outside, fending for himself. I can't ever remember him being inside the house.

Whenever mother and I left the house on her bicycle to go to the shops or see nana, the pup would run after us, but he couldn't keep up, bless him. He'd stop halfway, panting, and, do you know, we just kept on cycling.

With me being so young and mother caring for no-one but herself, the pup was pretty much neglected. He was just left to roam the streets and sleep outside.

I was only three years old when one day father put him in the car and dumped him in the countryside. I never really got a chance to bond with the pup, but it was a rotten thing to do. I never found out what became of him, but I don't suppose he survived long because there were no dog shelters back then.

My mother felt about as much love for me as my dad did for that dog - perhaps even less. I think if I'd have disappeared from the face of the earth it wouldn't have bothered her one bit.

Maybe she cared a little but couldn't show it. One time, she and father went on holiday to southern Ireland and left me behind at nana's house in Grove Hill. Father loved it out there because of the fishing.

It was great at nana and granddad's. I loved them dearly, but I missed my parents terribly.

Nana's food was just out of this world and her speciality was Spotted Dick, which she steamed in a pan with a Muslin cloth over the top. It was gorgeous.

I used to say to her: "Nana, if I come down on Friday will you do Spotted Dick?"

And she'd say: "Yes, if you go to the fish shop and get me a skate."

Skate was so rare back then that you'd have to order it the odd times they had it in.

When mum and dad got back from holiday two weeks later I ran up to mother and held out my arms to be embraced.

"Oh, mammy," I said.

"Oh, don't come near me," she said. "I've just had my hair done."

My nana's sister was in the house and she was disgusted.

"For God's sake, the child hasn't seen you in a fortnight," she said to mum.

But mother said nothing - she was more bothered about me messing her hair up. She was as cold as the night dews.

My fault, I suppose, was being born, which mother appeared to regard as the height of impertinence. It was an imposition she could never stomach, an intolerable duty of care which she knew she had to carry out, but decided for the most part that it would be easier to leave me in the care of others.

She taught me nothing about a woman's life, how to love or be loved, so I pinned all my hopes on my father. He was strict, but in my eyes, he was always high up on a pedestal, to be idolised. Yet they both had this hold on me which grew out of fear and blame, for things that were not my fault.

I got the feeling she blamed me for something, probably the fact that I'd been born. Maybe she thought I was in the way, that I'd curtailed her life and stopped her doing the things she used to do. She was a singer with the Charlie Amer's Band before she had me, doing the local pubs and clubs. When I popped out, she eventually stopped. Apparently, she had a very good voice.

When I got my first office job at 16, I got £4.7s 6d a week: that's four pounds, seven shillings and sixpence. That wasn't a lot of money even in those days, but mother demanded £4 for lodgings, which didn't leave me with much at all, but I wouldn't have dared argue with her. None of my friends were paying anywhere near that much to their parents for board and lodgings. I think they were giving their mams about £2, but where money was concerned, you didn't argue with mother.

When I got older my nana told me that when I was a baby, my mother took me to the shops in Grove Hill and came back without me. She'd left me in a pram outside a shop. Most mothers I know never take their eyes off their new baby. They can't stop looking at

14

them because they are so proud. My mother never felt an ounce of pride in me.

Instead, I reached out to others and started writing to a pen pal who, for her age, knew more about the birds and the bees than was good for her. One of her letters was particularly risqué and I was scared to death that mother would find it. I was petrified in case she thought that was how I talked to my friends.

My nana caught me reading the letter and said: "By, you've gone very white. Are you okay?"

"I'm fine, nana," I said.

If writing girly letters to pen pals was beyond the pale in mother's eyes, borrowing money was a sin worthy of eternal damnation. Once, a girl friend of mine came round to the house in Thorntree and asked me if I wanted to go to the pictures. I was on my own in the house as usual.

"But I have no money," I said. "Hang on, I think there's some money in the kitchen."

So I took some money from the kitchen drawer - I think it was about half a crown - and left a note for my parents, explaining that I'd borrowed a bit of money to go to the pictures with my friend Pat. We went to The Majestic, a short bus ride from our house. We had a nice time, but when I got back home, oh boy, did I get it. They called me a "thief" and made out like I'd just robbed the Bank of England or something.

"Well," I said, "thieves don't leave notes."

But they wouldn't have it. I was a thief, pure and simple. I went off to my bedroom and sobbed until my eyes turned red.

"How can I be a thief when I've left a note?" I thought.

But that was them; that's how they were with me. Mother, in particular, knew how to dish out blame and make me feel smaller than a grain of sand, though on this occasion I don't think she hit me because my father was there.

Boyfriends were a no-no too, even in my early teens. By the age of 14, I began to take notice of boys like all the girls my age, but God forbid I might bring one home. I got to know a lad who lived next-door to this family I used to babysit for. They were friends of my parents and lived in Redcar – far enough away, I hoped, for my parents never to find out about my flirtation with this lovely lad who I really fancied. He was a sort of boyfriend, I suppose, but in those days when you were 14 you acted like you were 14, not like today when the boys and girls are like 14 going on 25.

He came in one night while I was babysitting and we were just sat chatting, but I was petrified. I wasn't scared of him or what he might do, but I was terrified that my parents might call round and find me and the boy there.

"I don't feel well," I said to him. "I think you'll have to go home."

The poor lad was mortified: he hadn't done anything wrong and I had given him all the right signals up 'til then. He had no choice but to get up off the chair and walk out. He must have been so embarrassed, poor lad, and I felt so sorry for him, but I was more concerned about what my parents would do if they caught me chatting to a boy. I imagine they'd have called me a slut or a whore, because they're just the kind of words they'd have used. Oh yes.

I channelled all my thoughts and energies into study and came out top in virtually all my classes at junior school. I passed the 11-plus hands down and got a place at Kirby Grammar School for Girls, but I pretty much abandoned my studies there and then because once rock 'n' roll hit our shores, I couldn't care less. Life was never the same after Bill Haley & His Comets released 'Rock Around the Clock'. I was a big Elvis fan and loved Buddy Holly too. There was no time for schooling, not with Elvis and those hips, and my studies were thrown to the wind. I may have been a straight-A student in junior school, but at the grammar everyone was top of the class and I realised I'd been a big fish in a little pond.

Grammar school was split into two distinct camps depending on your rock 'n' roll taste: one lot, the 'Americans', liked Elvis, and the other lot, the 'Brits', like Tommy Steele. It was the heart-throb era and we all had idols, but I was never really into boys until I reached 15 or 16. None of them could compare with Elvis, so there seemed little point.

But then I met a boy called Gavin at the local youth club and I fell head over heels in love. He was a fine-looking lad and very canny - even my parents liked him. We stayed together for about a year-and-a-half, then the relationship just fizzled out. Gavin was a steady hand and ended up as a bank manager. Not dripping in personality, but given what was about to happen to me, maybe I should have stuck with him - or at least kept his phone number.

I had my teenage crushes like all the girls, but Gavin was my only serious boyfriend in the grammar-school days. Perhaps it was the fact that I wore glasses that kept the lads at bay, but I wasn't one of those girls that the boys chased. Far from it.

I looked a little prissy, secretarial even, in my woolly jumpers, cardigans and white blouses. I never followed fashion: I wore what I felt comfortable in. What you see the girls wearing nowadays, well, it just takes your breath away, doesn't it? Big girls with big legs wearing tiny skirts and tight tops with their tummies showing – even in January. To me, they just look ridiculous.

My only advantage was that I had naturally-curly red hair, but as a young girl I longed for straight hair. Curly hair was so unruly. And mine was very, very unruly.

I left school at 16 with just three O' Levels – a terrible underachievement and my father wallowed in despair. It would be no exaggeration to say he was mortified.

He presumed I'd be the star pupil once again, but my qualifications were less than mediocre. It was a shame on the family, a dreadful failure.

I wanted to be a hairdresser, but father said that no daughter of his who had been to grammar school was going to be crimping and curling hair for a living. He tried to get me into the bank (I think it was Barclays), but of course I failed maths miserably so that was a non-starter. I was more on the linguistic side: I loved English and French, which I was very good at. I can still speak conversational French even now.

With so few qualifications and no career prospects, I was a let-down to father whose frustration only deepened. But, as was the way in those days, I just sort of fell into a job. I was brought in for an interview at Dorman Long, then part of British Steel, and got an office job at the company's Britannia Works.

I met a guy there called Bill Yare and we got on very well. He was a really nice guy, dead quiet and a bit shy. He was nice to look at, but you could never call him handsome. He was just a very nice bloke and we talked a lot. We courted for about six months and went out to pubs and dances together, but Bill was 12 years older than me and he didn't go down too well with my parents. They were nice enough to him, but I think they were expecting Little Lord Fauntleroy or something for dear old Valerie.

There were about six or seven of us from the Britannia Works who used to go out for drinks and a dance. Me and Bill went out as a couple and one of my friends, Mary, was going out with one of Bill's mates. Bill was the perfect gentleman and would escort me home. The first night he came home with me, mother was on her best behaviour and was as nice as pie. Then, after he left, she turned to me and said: "He's too deep – you'll never know him."

That was mother: always quick to judge and often getting the wrong end of the stick. Bill may have been quiet and unassuming, but he was far from deep. He was a simple, uncomplicated man, but had a heart of gold and he was quite intelligent, dry-witted and uncomplaining. A bit of a softy, too.

I tried so hard to convince mother that Bill was a good guy, and then he goes and dumps me! He broke up with me 'cos he thought I was too young. He fancied a girl called Carol, but she wouldn't have looked twice at him.

I was heartbroken, but I moved on and stayed friends with his mum Edie, who was just a sweetheart. I had other boyfriends but nothing serious. I didn't miss Bill, who eventually became more of a brother to me than a friend.

I ended up transferring to Dorman Longs' Cleveland Works because I wanted to be a telephonist. I had an excellent phone manner and thought the job was made for me because I had experience on the phones and in the steel industry. I spent two years at Cleveland working the phones and then Bill turns up there. A little awkward, perhaps, but we were still mates.

I knew Bill still had the eye for me, but I was just a baby in his eyes and he left me alone. We parted ways again when I left the Cleveland office and I got a job at the Head Wrightson machine company, working in the print room.

One day, not long into the job, some male staff came in and were trying to get something printed, but it wouldn't print.

One of these blokes said: "Oh, it probably needs servicing."

"Oh, so do I," I said. "I'm so tired."

I told my parents when I got home and, oh, did I get it.

"Do you know that they service a cow?" one of them said.

It completely baffled me.

They explained to me, in no uncertain terms, that when they put a cow to a bull it was called servicing.

"I don't know what you're talking about," I pleaded.

How should I have known that an innocent remark about servicing a bloody printer and feeling tired could be conflated with sex between a cow and a randy bull?

It was absurd, it was utterly ridiculous, but that's how their minds worked, and everything I ever did or said was twisted beyond recognition. And to think what I knew about them years later. They weren't puritans – that's for sure.

To connotate sexual meaning from an innocent remark about a bloody printer is of course truly bizarre (never mind a little creepy), but they were the master manipulators, and this was a deliberate attempt at intimidation. By God, it worked. They always knew which buttons to press.

My father only had to say something once and I knew. But he was only ever verbal: he never, ever raised a hand to me. It was mother who dished out the slaps and sometimes I think I may even have felt a clenched fist. She had a vicious tongue and could cut you down in a sentence.

I ended up ditching the printer room when I was 19 and became a nanny. I got a position with a family in Richmond who ran a pub called The Black Bull in the pretty village of Moulton. I lived in the cottage opposite the pub that the family owned. I think I went for this job so I could leave home.

It wasn't a bad life. I looked after three children during the week and Bill and his mate Eric used to visit at weekends, when we'd have lock-ins at the pub. Mum and dad would drive over occasionally and have a drink with me.

The kids - Diana, Charles and baby Sarah - were canny, and I got the odd day off when I'd go into Darlington to get my hair cut. I was a good nanny; I had that maternal instinct. I stuck at it for a year until I took very ill with food poisoning and had to go back home. I craved my independence, but I was so ill I just wanted to go home. I returned to my parents and never went back. It was a fateful decision because if I'd have stayed in Richmond, I would never have met the man who turned my life upside down.

For a woman my age, it was a terrible drag being back at home, but it gave me time to get over the food poisoning, reacquaint myself with some old friends and go look for another job. It didn't take long to find one and it was really quite a bobby's job. I became receptionist at The Grand Hotel in Hartlepool, the biggest and one of the best hotels in the North East which had become home to a boatload of Americans who were working on the North Sea oil rigs. The Americans worked two weeks on, then a week off, which they spent carousing in the pubs and clubs of Hartlepool. They were loud, they were loaded and they were good fun. Up for anything.

Hartlepool was far from a hip town - backwards in many ways - but the Yanks added a dash of colour and excitement to the place. They wore flash clothes, had perfect teeth and smiled a lot more than the Hartlepudlian men, who were a bit dowdy, lugubrious and generally snaggle-toothed. The ladies loved the Americans: it was like World War Two all over again.

In the mid-60s, Hartlepool wasn't ready for an American invasion: the Hartlepudlians were the 'monkey-hangers', after all. The story has gone down in folklore, but many swear it's true. During the Napoleonic Wars of the 1800s, the wreckage of a French vessel, which had been caught up in a storm, washed up on the town's shores. A bunch of local fishermen, fearing an invasion, surveyed the wreckage suspecting espionage, but found only a very wet and very dejected monkey which they were convinced was a spy, presumably because he was dressed in military-style uniform to amuse the French shipmen.

Legend has it that the local fishermen, who had never seen a Frenchman - and had presumably never seen a monkey - actually interrogated the poor creature and held a trial on the beach. They decided that the monkey was a French spy and must die. They sentenced him to death by hanging. Again, this is only anecdotal, but apparently the monkey was hanged from the mast of a fishing boat.

As far as I know, no American was ever mistaken for a monkey, nor hanged – they were generally far too good-looking, well-groomed and not nearly as hirsute.

In 2002, many years after the Americans had left the North East, a monkey was elected mayor of Hartlepool. H'Angus the Monkey, Hartlepool FC's mascot, got a £53,000-a-year job as the town's First Citizen promising "free bananas for schoolchildren". He got thrown out of two away games – once for simulating sex with a woman steward in Scunthorpe and another time for doing something unspeakable with an inflatable doll at a game with Blackpool.

We girls had a good time with the Americans; they were fun guys to be around. They were friendly and effortlessly charming. Nearly all handsome and all proper gentleman. I had the time of my life 'cos they were loaded and they were generous to a fault. All their hotel expenses were covered by the oil company which left them loads of money to spend on us English girls. I got to know three or four of them very well indeed – I was no angel. It was the 1960s after all, but I wasn't a hedonist or anything like that. I just liked a good time like all the girls.

Me and another girl called Sylvia who worked at The Grand went out with them for a jive and a good night out. There were lots of free drinks, lots of laughs and much flirtation. We'd never had it so good. For us girls, having grown up around men who wore cloth caps, oil-stained uniforms and reared whippets, it was irresistible. English girls had a good time with the Americans after the war. It was mostly about the money, but they also made us laugh; they made us feel glamorous and not so dowdy. My friend Sylvia actually married one and moved to Florida with him. I never imagined for a second I'd get romantically involved with any of them - and then along came Jim.

Chapter 3

The Trap

He wasn't especially handsome. His clothes were down-home, plain, but there was something about James Olan Bumbard which I found irresistible.

He was a rigid, unrevealing sort of person, the type who never betrayed his emotions. He was straight-backed, a picture of calm and self-assurance. It wasn't arrogance (or so I believed), but to others he appeared remote, not worth getting to know. That sort of guy. Best left to himself.

He was pretty much shunned by the other Americans and ignored by the English girls, but for some reason I was intrigued. His aloofness beguiled me: I wanted to know more about this man who was so unlike his compatriots, who were all noise, razzle-dazzle and up for anything.

Jim was quiet and didn't drink, and he had dark hair which I liked very much. He'd come back from the rigs and quietly slink off to his hotel room when all the other Yanks came crashing home in the small hours with a girl on each arm and reeking of liquor. I watched this pale shadow of a man from my vantage on the reception desk. He struck me as a loner, barely noticeable to anyone else, but, to me, a mystery that just had to be unravelled.

He wore his suits well and was of a generally tidy appearance. There was nothing remotely eye-catching to the casual observer, but, to me, he had this allure and I must admit I was transfixed. I kept trying to catch his eye as he wandered into the restaurant and offered up a smile as he breezed past me on reception. He was polite and courteous, but never once glanced over at me; never struck up much of a conversation. I just put that down to shyness.

I suppose I fell for this American because he was so un-American. There's that old saying about the ugly fish attracting the best mates because they stand out in a crowd. Jim was tall and dark, but he was no handsome stranger by any estimation. Yet he had a certain detached composure that could bring a girl to her knees.

This was a man who didn't drink, gamble or swear. And remember this was at a time when Americans in Teesside were given a licence to do pretty much as they pleased.

My attempts at subtle flirtation were met with a stonewall of what appeared to be utter disinterest, but I wasn't going to give up on this man. He had to be mine.

I noticed I was taking much greater care getting ready for work in a morning, checking and re-checking my appearance in the mirror, doing up and then re-doing my ruby-red hair, then doing it again. I always made sure my attire was just so, but he never gave me the slightest encouragement; not once did I feel like me and this man would one day take the altar together. It seemed not even a remote possibility.

He struck me as the archetypal Southern gent, all good manners and "Thank you, ma'am". That was just what he did.

But there was never a hint of flirtation. Indeed, the conversation rarely got past the odd request for room service or the changing of a light bulb. I was just pleasant with him and he with me, but there was no sparkle to begin with.

And then things just started to happen, not noticeably at first, but then I realised he was starting to make a beeline for my desk when he returned from the rigs. Just small talk at first and "How ya doing, ma'am?", that sort of thing. But it gradually began to dawn on me that this quiet American had designs on me. After a time, I realised I was thinking about him all the time: on the way to work, at work, on the way home from work, when I got home, when I went to bed, and first thing in the morning. It just sort of crept up on me, unbidden, but I couldn't get him off my mind.

At The Grand, you worked from 3 o'clock in the afternoon to 11 o'clock at night. You slept over in the staff quarters and then you were on duty the next morning from 7am to 3pm, so you were basically 24 hours there and 24 hours off. One day he asked me to go to the pictures and suddenly we were an item. I think it was a James Bond film.

Jim held my hand for the first time halfway through the spy film as I was quietly munching popcorn. Afterwards, I offered to show him around Middlesbrough and told him my dad had a business in town.

We started going out to nightclubs and it began to dawn on me that we were without doubt a couple, perhaps even heavily in love. He wasn't a bad dancer, but nothing out of the ordinary: I'd seen better even in the dance halls of Middlesbrough.

One night, not too long after we started dating, I took him home to meet my parents because I felt the time was right. I felt sure they'd like him, though you never knew with those two. If they didn't like you, they didn't like you, and they'd make no bones about it. No reason was required.

I was quite apprehensive, but I needn't have been: they thought he was marvellous, the bee's knees. I mean they really, really liked him, and I thought that if two of the most judgemental people in the world think he's great, I must be onto something. He really was like a ray of light.

My parents fell for him straight away, so I kept bringing him home and it was always the same open-arms welcome, even from mother, who had all the emotional sensitivity of a Medieval executioner. They even let him stay the night when I was at work. Ye Gods!

I'd go back to work at 3 o'clock the next day and I'd miss him terribly. I'd never experienced anything like it. I missed him so much I ached, and all because I knew I wasn't going to see him for another 24 hours. A full day without Jim's company was like the worst kind of torture.

I was in love, I suppose; at least I felt like I was. I was really taken by him, despite his ordinariness. There was nothing flashy about him, there was no swagger; he was just an 'Average Joe', or so I thought.

There was no physical intimacy at first - not that he didn't try. He was the perfect gentleman and may as well have had a halo around his head as far as my parents were concerned. He was so well-behaved over here you couldn't fault him if you tried. He was courteous to a tee and so well-mannered, particularly around my parents. He called my father "Sir" and my mother "Ma'am". He called me by my Sunday name – Valerie, or 'Valer-ee'.

There was no doubt about it - old Jimbo had my mother and father well and truly hooked. And me of course.

If Jim was the epitome of Southern charm and impeccable manners, the other Americans were bawdy and cheap, in a friendly sort of way. I even got kind of snobbish about it and told my girl friends that my American was nothing like the ones they knew. I was in a good position to judge because I'd been with three or four Americans who stayed at the hotel, and while they gave me a good time and were all nice fellows, none of them could ever compare with Jim. I may have looked like a picture of studious innocence, but I knew how to have a good time, and good times were there to be had.

I did think for a moment that Jim was too good to be true, but I cast that ridiculous notion aside and didn't give it another thought. And I'd caught him just at the right time: twenty-six is a good age for a man to marry a girl with aspirations to a family life. There was a six-year age gap between us, but that didn't bother me 'cos I was quite mature for my years, intellectually as well as physically, and it all felt so natural.

There was no doubt about it, I'd fallen head over heels and within three months we were married. When he proposed, I never gave it a second thought.

We got married at the Registry Office in Middlesbrough in January 1966, and there was no doubt in my mind that everything would turn out rosy. Of course, I had no inkling that I had committed myself to damnation; a fate so horrible I'm still feeling the repercussions to this day.

The only people there to witness my biggest mistake in life were my parents, my friend Kathy - the maid-of-honour - and my uncle Tom, who was Jim's best man. Uncle Tom thought the sun shone out of Jim's backside, as did most people, to be fair.

I took his courtesies, his smile, his gentility, at face value and saw nothing in the man that could cloud my judgement. Looking back now, I think that when he saw where my parents lived, and what my father did for a living, he thought he was onto a good thing. We'd moved to Brookfield, one of the nicest parts of Middlesbrough, the kind of place working-class people aspired to if they had a bit of money. And with enough hard work or a savvy business brain, or both, many were able to make a good living for themselves because there was work aplenty. This was in the days when you could finish one job on the Friday and start another job on the Monday. It sounds ludicrous now, but back then there really was work for everyone. I left grammar school with barely any qualifications; I was a wasted talent, yet I'd landed a relatively well-paid job as soon as I left school. And now I had a husband I worshipped, I'd just left The Grand to go work for my father and I had no financial worries whatsoever.

Jim and I moved into a house together in Middlesbrough, but it was only rented because his plan was always to return to the States, way down in Louisiana. We'd only been in the house a few days when Kathy, my best woman at the wedding, dropped by for a sort of house-warming. Me and Kathy were really close friends and had been on holiday together in Belgium in '63. We had worked together at Head Wrightson and stayed friends ever since.

It was a Sunday and I'd invited my parents round for tea. After a pleasant meal my parents left, but on this occasion I didn't accompany them to the front door to wave them off. For some reason - and I couldn't put my finger on exactly why - I didn't want to leave Jim alone with Kathy, so I just said "bye" to my parents as they went out of the lounge door. He'd never given me a reason to think he might do something like make a pass at my best friend, or mess around with other girls, but there was just something that day that made me think: "I'm not leaving him in this room with my friend."

Maybe it was women's intuition. We'd only been married a couple of weeks, but already, something must have been stirring inside me. No doubt my subconscious was screaming with dire warnings of what was to come, but I took no notice. When all's said and done, I knew I was deeply in love with this man, which quickly banished any pernicious thoughts.

A few days after the Sunday get-together, mother rebuked me for not going to the door to wave them off.

"You weren't very nice that night," she said, or rather hissed.

There was one other glint of suspicion regarding Jim which to any rational mind would have set the alarm bells ringing straight away, but I suppose I was so in love that I'd turn a blind to anything. He'd brought a framed photo of himself from the States. I didn't pay it much attention until one day I picked it up and read the inscription: 'To (a woman whose name I don't recall), with all my love.'

Bizarrely, Jim gave it to me as if he were handing me a billet-doux. Even more bizarrely, I didn't suspect a thing.

"Poor bloke," I thought.

I must have assumed it was a lost love or someone who had died, but it's very odd that I didn't ask any questions.

A few weeks after we moved into the rented house, Jim said his time on the rigs was up and it was time to go back to America. We agreed that I would follow him out a few weeks later.

He packed his bags before February was out and from the moment that man left the Tarmac at Teesside Airport, my heart ached because I knew it would be another couple of weeks before I flew out to be with him. I yearned for him, dreamed about him; even dreaded the possibility that some cataclysmic event might prevent us being reunited. Those few weeks without him nearly drove me insane. It was like the feeling you get when you've been to a great party and everyone has left, leaving you behind with only a scotch and the bartender for company.

I counted down the days to departure with all the desperation of a smitten woman with nothing to do but read books and indulge her own anxieties. I simply couldn't wait to get across the Atlantic.

In truth, I'd have followed him across the world if he'd wanted me to. I had the confidence and the fearlessness of a smart, 20-year-old, love struck woman in her prime, and the thought of leaving Middlesbrough behind didn't bother me one bit. Besides, I'd had enough of the smog and the smokestacks. America was all bright and shiny and new and it was the home of rock 'n' roll, after all.

I yearned to see what the rest of the world looked like and when Jim came along it felt like heaven's doors had opened to me. I dreamed of picket fences, drive-in movies and sipping pink lemonade in the sunshine. Little did I know that the dark clouds had drifted in as soon as I laid eyes on him. The darkness had descended the very first time he walked through the doors of The Grand hotel and I never knew it. I saw only the glow of his halo.

I ran into this hell with open arms and all the excitement of a girl in the first flush of romance. I packed my bags and told my parents that I was leaving. They never really said much; that wasn't their way. I just think they thought it was a foregone conclusion.

Finally, departure day arrived, and it was like Manna from heaven. My parents drove me to Teesside Airport and I was so excited I couldn't stop smiling. My heart thumped, but there was no trepidation. Spring was just around the corner and ahead lay America, the New World, and Jim!

My man was waiting for me on the other side of the ocean and I was sure that he was just as excited as I was. I imagined he'd be waiting anxiously for the phone to ring so he could dash to the airport and scoop me up in his arms. I imagined lots of things in those days, none of which had anything to do with reality.

Mother showed me all the warmth of a block of ice when they dropped me off at the airport. It was as if she was dropping me off for a weekend camp with the Guides. My dad showed a degree of fatherly attentiveness but nowhere near enough for me to question the logic of my decision.

I boarded the plane confident in the knowledge that I'd made the right decision and that my future belonged to Jim and America. Nor did I have any doubt that I was carrying his child: I'd missed two periods, so by the time I got to America I knew I was pregnant.

I got a connecting flight at London Heathrow but had to wait several hours. I flew out to Washington, then to Birmingham, Alabama, then on to Atlanta, Georgia, then to New Orleans where Jim met me – drunk out of his mind.

This man who had barely touched a drop of liqueur in England was now rolling drunk, befuddled and seemingly a completely different creature to the one I had fallen in love with in England. I was gobsmacked: I'd never seen him in any such kind of state.

I was expecting a gleaming knight; instead I was met by a falling-down drunk who stank of hooch, reeked of gut-rot. It was an almighty shock; I didn't know how to react, but I put it down to an aberration. Naively, I even thought he had got drunk to calm his nerves because he was so excited to see me.

There was this bloke with him who had driven him to New Orleans. I had no idea who he was, but he was certainly no edifying presence. A loutish sort, perhaps, but I don't know: it was night-time and I was very tired from the jetlag.

We piled into his car and drove out to Morgan City on the Gulf of Mexico. We checked in at the Hotel Royal where Jim and I made love. It was heaven.

Jim was a good lover even when stone drunk. The only thing that spoiled it a little were the cockroaches I spotted crawling on the ceiling.

We stayed at the hotel for maybe a few months and despite Jim's personality being totally at odds with his charm and diffidence in the UK, I still had no doubt I had made the right decision. I put his boorishness and his drinking down to early-marriage jitters.

I cut him some slack, but he started hitting me within weeks, and it was always when he had been drinking. I mean literally knocking me off my feet. And all the while I had to work on reception at the hotel to pay for our room 'cos Jim didn't lift a finger.

Morgan City was the kind of town, and this hotel was that sort of place, where people stayed when they came off the rigs 'cos it was right on the gulf, so it was always full of transient people. I got the reception job after telling the owner, a nice man who looked sort of Italian, that I had experience in the field. There was an older lady called Gladys who worked reception with me and we got on well.

It wasn't a very nice hotel and its amenities were basic to the core. The Deep South would indeed be very different from anything I had ever experienced before. It was a place with its own rules, a country within a country, and the man I had fallen in love with was about to teach me everything I needed to know about playing by the rules. Oh yes.

Chapter 4

Night Flit

I'm in the United States of America with a husband I do not know and who appears to have no intention of holding down any kind of gainful employment.

It's a mystery. He'd travelled 4,500 miles to find work in England, but he won't lift a finger here in his own country, where there's surely work aplenty.

He crossed an ocean to work on the rigs, but now he just drank. It began to dawn on me that perhaps he was just bone idle.

I wanted a husband who could provide, but he looked to me to bring in the money. I just hoped he'd eventually get his act together and get some more work on the rigs or something. Surely he'll want work if a child comes along? It's a man's natural inclination, after all.

If I am indeed with child (as I am certain I am), then my husband's got to change pretty drastically and pretty soon, or there's gonna be some mighty upheaval somewhere down the line and he might even sink us.

Yet our daily routine remains the same: I work reception for a pittance and Jim goes out to God knows where, to do God knows what, with God knows who. And he always come back drunk.

I'm in a strange land with few friends and my husband, whom my parents and I had down as a saint, shows all the signs of being a hopeless alcoholic. A violent one to boot.

The attacks began within weeks. The first time, he'd been out and got steaming drunk and returned to our hotel room reeking of liquor. All I said was: "Where've you been?"

And that's all it took. Wham! The first attack.

He was 6ft, a foot taller than me. His hand came down with an open palm and struck me on the chin. I went flying across the room. I saw stars; I didn't know what had happened. I had no inkling before this.

I was bawling my eyes out; I was in shock. I couldn't believe that he could do that to me. He got down on his knees and said: "Honey, I'm so sorry. I'll never do it again."

That would become a familiar refrain after an attack – and there would be plenty.

Our lives at the hotel became a weekly pattern of monotonous work (on my part), routine violence (on Jim's), and boredom. I was quietly disturbed by how quickly I'd settled into this life of casual domestic violence so soon into the marriage, as if I'd been expecting it all along (which, of course, I hadn't). It was becoming clear that booze was the catalyst, yet he appeared almost tee-total in England.

One night he came back to our room in a filthy mood, rotten drunk, boozed up to his eyelids. He hit me as soon as he walked in, but this time I hit him back. He was so mad and so drunk that it was easy. I pushed him and he fell against the radiator in the bedroom. He stayed there all night 'cos he'd fallen into a deep, drunken sleep, snoring his head off, and the next day he had all these red stripes down his back where the heat of the radiator columns had left marks running down his spine.

He was telling everybody, sort of jokingly, that it was his wife who had done this to him. Only he forgot to mention that he hit me first.

I try really hard to make new friends and make some sense of this new world, but it's not easy in a transient community like this, because people are there one minute and gone the next. There's little time to form bonds, but there was this one guy called Floyd who came over from Texas to look for work on the rigs. Apparently, he had a big ranch over there, but there'd been floods and he'd lost everything. He'd come over to Louisiana in the hope of making some money, so he could return to Texas and maybe get his ranch back up and running, but he couldn't read or write.

I took pity on Floyd, a fat little feller who was such a nice bloke but seemed completely bereft. I told him I would teach him how to read and used to sit with him for hours, reading books and newspapers and magazines, even the pamphlets from the stand on the reception desk.

31

One day, Floyd and I went to the laundrette just down the road, but just as we were about to go in, I spotted a sign in the corner of the window which read: 'Whites Only Here'.

I thought they meant 'white-coloured clothes only', so we walked in and I stuffed my whites into the washing machine near the sign on the window. Floyd was in hysterics, but I had no idea why and continued shoving my whites into the drum.

"What are you doing?" he said.

"It says 'whites only' here," I replied.

Floyd explained to me that in fact the sign barred coloured people from entering. I was shocked, then embarrassed, and finally angry. This was indeed a strange country.

I had grown up in a town where you didn't really see anything other than white faces. I think you saw the occasional Jamaican, but most black people ended up in London. There wasn't a hint of racial tension in Middlesbrough in the 1950s and 60s because there were no racial divisions to speak of. It was virtually all white.

And suddenly I'm thrown into a kind of Apartheid state, in which human beings, purely by dent of their colour, are barred from entering a laundrette to do something as simple as wash their clothes. Good grief.

Floyd was dead canny; really nice. We lost touch after we left the hotel, but I do hope he got that ranch back up and running, or at least found some work to feed his family. I taught him what I could in the confines of a halfway house which was about as conducive to educational endeavour as a bawdy house on the Sunset Strip.

One night I was sat behind reception when the cops burst in with their guns flashing and arrested a guy. I don't know what he'd done, but it was terrifying. Just another transient who disappeared into the night and was never seen again.

This land - or at least this hotel, and this city - was beginning to scare me, and I was starting to do what I never expected to: pine for home. Not for my mum or dad; not for Bill, nor my nana and grandad. But I was dying for some mashed potato and gravy.

The hotel was bed only, no food, so Jim and I used to go to a café next-door for eggs (sunny-side up), crawfish (a Louisiana speciality) and southern fried chicken.

Other than breakfast in the café, we'd order takeaways. It was pretty good fare and we also had Mary's Chicken Shack, which was a bit like Kentucky Fried Chicken, only better in my opinion. It was gorgeous; proper southern fried chicken. I can still smell and taste it today. Jim and I used to feast on it.

The Crayfish, or Crawfish, was brought in fresh from a guy who worked on the boats on the gulf. They were a bit like lobster, but I thought tastier.

But still I craved my mash. One day, around the time of my 21st birthday, Jim introduced me to this guy and his wife who invited us round for a roast lunch on Easter Sunday. The guy's wife and I had been out shopping together and got on quite well, and I told her I was dying for some mashed potato and gravy.

"Come to our house on Sunday for lunch and I'll cook you a proper beef dinner with gravy and mashed potatoes," she said.

I couldn't wait. We went to their house not far from the hotel and had this lovely roast dinner. The mash and gravy were delicious, just divine. They made the gravy nice and thick, just like over here. It was just like being sat around the table back home in Brookfield. And Jim was on his best behaviour, all manners and courtesy, like the Jim of old. It was a very pleasant time.

And then all four of us went out to a bar in town following lunch. We were sat round this table and I didn't know it at the time, but apparently there was this guy who couldn't take his eyes off me. Jim clocked it straight away and walked up to this guy to confront him.

Jim said to him: "If you see something you like, throw a dime at it."

So the guy threw a dime at our table, which meant he'd accepted the challenge of a fight and suddenly he and Jim were squaring up in the middle of the bar, like two stags in mating season. Jim punched him and within seconds it was utter chaos: everyone piled in. Fists were flying, chairs whistled through the air, crashing to the floor in splinters and broken stumps. And there's my Jim wrestling this guy on the bar. My husband was clearly getting the better of him. My guy was a hard feller and despite the mayhem, I thought: "Well he must love me if he'd fight for me."

It was a mass brawl, just like you'd see in the Westerns. My lady friend and I legged it out the bar. It was getting out of control and I knew what that fella was going through because Jim had done the same to me. Never went to that place again.

The hotel was the first time I'd ever encountered cockroaches and, my God, it was crawling with these creatures. When you got up in the middle of the night and turned the lights on, they'd be scuttling across the walls. I'll never forget that sound. And they were so big!

Every now and again these guys would come into the hotel and squirt this stuff at them. It was some kind of pesticide. I think it was DDT.

It was like I'd walked quite willingly into a nightmarish Southern cliché: violence, drink, deeply-suspect characters and oversized insects which woke you up at night and made the most horrible sound.

One night, after I finished my shift on reception, Jim told me to pack my things: we were leaving. God knows what he'd done. I knew he must have done something, but I didn't know what. In any case, we were on our way.

"We're leaving," he said.

He was in such a rush to leave I barely had time to pack. I asked no questions, but it was the first time that I thought: "What the hell's he done? Has he robbed someone or something?"

We went in the middle of the night like two cat burglars fleeing the scene of a crime. Some guy gave us a lift to the Greyhound bus station in Morgan City and that was the end of the Hotel Royal. Jim said we were going to his mother's, which was 250 miles north in Mansfield, Louisiana, a country-hick sort of place. The nearest big town to Mansfield was Shreveport 36 miles away, where the airport was.

Mansfield, I knew, was stuck in the middle of nowhere. The only other thing I knew about the place was that the film producer Joshua Logan, who directed Paint Your Wagon and South Pacific, had grown up there. The only thing I knew about Louisiana was that it was sandwiched between Texas and Mississippi.

We were just another transient couple squashed into seats alongside dozens of drifters and down-and-outs. The journey took about six hours with a couple of stops along the way. I spent most of my time sleeping on Jim's shoulder. I don't know why, but I felt like a fugitive.

It was on the Greyhound bus that I first came across segregation. When black people got on, they had to stand, even if there were vacant seats. I was shocked. To me it was strange because people were people, no matter what their colour or background.

We stopped at a couple of service stations along the way and at one of the stops I had my first proper American beef burger. Oh, it was heaven. I couldn't believe how good it tasted.

Over in England in the 60s, it was just a burger in a bun, with no trimmings, but over here it had lettuce, gherkins, tomato sauce. Delicious.

I presume Jim must have stolen something before our midnight flit because he had the money to buy me the burger – a rare show of generosity.

We arrived in Mansfield in the early hours and stayed in a motel, just like the one in Psycho, except here the staff were very welcoming and pleasant. Yet I felt frightened, out of my depth and a little lost. I just thought: "This is my life now."

I was 5,000 transatlantic miles away from home, so I couldn't just jump on a bus and go home. And I was only just married: it seemed only yesterday that Jim was all sweetness and light. In any case, in those days you made your bed and you had to lie in it. I'd already resigned myself to this fate, but it would have been nice to know what exactly I was lying next to.

The next morning, Jim rang his mum to tell her we were here and that we'd be coming over. We got a taxi to his mum's house, which was basically a wooden shack which looked like it hadn't been painted in years. It had a front porch and was crawling with cockroaches. Jim's mum, Fanny, was a dab hand at killing them and very house-proud, but they kept coming back.

Fanny Bumbard was a widow who had raised four boys largely on her own. It's hard to imagine just how difficult a task that must have been, but I was soon to find out. She also had a daughter, Alice Fay.

Fanny was a gentle, homely sort of woman and very friendly. Her welcome was warm and sincere. She put her arms around me and gave me a big hug. She welcomed me into the family with open arms. I liked her instantly.

She introduced me to Alice Fay, who lived just down the road and seemed a very nice young woman; perfectly pleasant. She and her mother seemed very glad to see me and Fanny cooked us a nice breakfast, which Jim and I wolfed down because we were so hungry.

Mansfield was a dry town, a rural outpost where no alcohol was allowed. God knows what Jim was doing in a 'dry' town, but I assumed he'd found a way around the injunction, just like he found a way around most things.

There was a small highway running through the town and a gas station opposite Fanny's shack, but other than that, nothing much to speak of. Just shacks, one after the other, dotted geometrically along Route 4. Fanny's mother, who was in her 90s, lived next-door, but at quite some remove, and you had to go over a path to get there.

We were given a bedroom at the front of the house and that first night I remember thinking what I had let myself into.

The shack was a tiny, wooden structure. A dull grey shanty. There was a front room on the left, which I suppose you would call a living room; a front bedroom on the right, which me and Jim were in; a kitchen to the back left of the square hut; and to the back right was a bedroom that everybody used, with a bathroom behind it. There was just a shutter for a front door; like a screen, with no lock, just a little hook on it. Anyone could have walked in, but they had nothing so there was nothing to steal anyway.

You went through the lounge into the kitchen, which was tiny. There were mice scuttering about all over the place and you could hear them scurrying across the rafters. I'd be sat there with a bat in my hand waiting for them to run out of this little hole in the wall. I'd try to hit them, but they were so lightning fast it was useless.

There was no back yard, and next to the shanty was another house which, standing at a right angle to Fanny's shack, stared right down on us. There was a bathroom of sorts and they all had a front porch with a rocking chair.

Jim's mum told me all about her church and her faith. She did a lot of work for the Methodist Church and was a devoted Christian. She told me I could call her "mum".

I'm sat here with this lovely woman and I look over at Jim shovelling a spoonful of beans into his belly, and I start wondering how on earth she could have produced him.

Fanny's husband, Charles, had died years ago and she'd evidently taken on the demands of five children with little support, but without complaint.

Jim had three brothers - Aubrey, Charlie and Oneal. One of them (I don't remember which) was in prison; another had walked out one day and never came back; and another was barred from the town.

Jim's mother offered me these little nuggets of family history over a rocking chair and lemonade on the porch. I thought back to my initial suspicions about Jim, my concerns about leaving him alone with Kathy, but his mother's warmth and hospitality were so effusive that I decided to put these worries out of my mind, for now at least.

In the early days, I never heard her criticise any of her sons. I'd been there only a few days, but it was already becoming clear that I'd married into a wholly dysfunctional family and entered a quite dangerous situation – and it was all of my own volition. I'd travelled thousands of miles and got an airline ticket - one-way!

Yet I still held out hopes for this husband of mine, who was presently scoffing bacon and beans over the kitchen table. Besides, he had at least paid for my airline ticket, or so he told me. According to Jim, he'd sent a cheque for $1,000 to my father. It strikes me as quite odd now that I didn't smell a rat. After all, Jim was stony broke and lived off state benefits.

I'd heard all the salutary tales about Southern life, but I had left Britain with an open mind, perhaps out of excitement, perhaps out of blind optimism, and banished such thoughts as sweeping generalisations. The people seemed okay, though the only ones I knew well were the family and some of the neighbours. I did note, however, that none of the family went to church except Fanny.

Yet here I was with my new family, and, apart from those who were in jail or had done a runner, they all lived on the same highway and they all kept chickens and geese.

Jim's grandma had a 'back yard', as they called their gardens. She was a lovely old lady. Apparently, her first husband was a drummer boy in the civil war – or at least, that's what Jim told me.

She called me Vera, which I thought was very funny. Every night she'd say: "Vera, go and get the geese in."

She had a black maid from Social Service who I guess would have been in her early 30s. The maid had children to feed and on such a meagre wage she did her best, bless her. She came to grandma's shack every day to clean and cook for her. The maid was a sweet lady who was always smiling despite a hard life and menial work for next to nothing.

I made a point of chatting to her because I liked her very much. She'd been assigned to Jim's grandma and every time she came round to the house I'd make her a coffee and we'd sit on the front porch, having a natter. We became quite good friends, but one day Jim came home and found me talking to her on the porch. He knocked me from one end of the house to the other for talking to a "nigger".

I cried myself to sleep that night and thought back to Middlesbrough as Jim slept off the booze. Of course, my home town had its own racists and bigots, but it was a haven of tolerance and acceptance compared with this place.

Even the nice whites had black maids if they were on Social Service. Every last one of them, if they required help from the state and no matter how disreputable, were able to call upon the authorities for a black cook or a cleaner as if it was their God-given right. They all took the maids for granted and didn't pay them any mind. This was completely new territory for me. I felt very uneasy.

And remember this was a deeply-religious town which purported to live by the Christian ethos of loving thy fellow man. I didn't see a lot of love around, but perhaps my perception was a little skewed because I was Jim's bedfellow. And Jim was most certainly a man of these parts.

Jim's sister Alice Fay had a 14-year-old daughter called Alice Marie and a younger daughter whose name I can't remember. Her husband, James, was a hard-working family man, very pleasant. They had a smallholding out back where they kept chickens. Theirs was the last shack at the end of the highway and after that there were just trees and open grassland – the wilds, where all the "Goddamn niggers" and "white trash" lived, away from all the "good white people" of the town.

They were the nice side of the family, the antithesis of Jim and his good-for-nothing brothers. Jim's mum and Alice Fay told me that one of the brothers (not Jim) once took a young girl into some woods and raped her. I'm pretty sure I know which brother it was, but not sure enough to name him.

I assume the matter must have gone to the courts, but I'm not sure what came of it. What I do know is that he was barred from the town and when I arrived, barely anyone in the family mentioned his name, though he did turn up now and again to see his mother. He was always steaming drunk when he came back; I remember that much. I was petrified of him but didn't dare show it. I always felt very uneasy around him. He looked to me like a proper white-trash hillbilly – and a dangerous one at that.

Chapter 5

Everything Wilts and Sweats

I was pregnant with Jim's child, but the beatings only got worse. He seemed to delight in it.

Once we were sat in his mother's and he picked his boot up off the floor. He was just about to hit me with it when his mother walked in.

"If you touch that girl I'll call the sheriff," she said.

Jim put the boot down and shot me a look which sent a chill down my spine. It was a face contorted with rage, full of hate, but he backed off and I thanked God for his mother.

For the life of me, I can't remember what had lit his fuse, but he was ready to give me a good hiding with that big old leather boot, and he surely would have laced me had it not been for dear old Fanny.

I was shaking with fear and crying again, but I knew that while Fanny was there I was okay. It was when she was away that the beatings occurred. And they always coincided with Jim getting his Sociality Security cheque – and his booze.

Since I'd been there, he hadn't done a day's work, and when the benefit cheque arrived he'd go on a drinking binge and blow all his cash on whisky and beer, and then attack me. He always attacked me when he was drunk, but when he was sober he was okay, almost gentlemanly. Fanny knew what was going on and did her utmost to protect me.

I was five months' pregnant, but Jim didn't seem to care a jot about this child that I was carrying inside me. I got the feeling that the beatings were a calculated assault on our child.

Not once during those first five months of pregnancy did I seek medical attention because I couldn't afford it. Jim had no money and he wouldn't have handed it over anyway, even if he had the riches of Solomon. The child, for him, was clearly an unwanted distraction.

Finally, about halfway through the pregnancy, Jim's mother made me go to see a doctor in Mansfield. I think it was the one she used.

I agreed to go. It would have been remiss and neglectful of me not to seek medical attention when the child is four months from birth.

There were two doors at the doctor's surgery: one had a sign saying 'White' and the other had a door saying 'Black'. I went in through the 'white' one and I was met by a black nurse!

They said I was too small to deliver the child myself; that I'd need a Caesarean. That was the only time I went.

One night, I was trying to put the geese away and Jim came out with a broom with the handle sticking out. I turned around and there he was, wielding this sweeper and grinning. Oh, good God, surely he wasn't going to come at me with his child inside my womb?

He was holding the broom like a battering ram and thrust it towards my pregnant stomach, missing the bump by inches. He jabbed again – a hair's breadth from my unborn child. I began to cry and begged him to stop, but Jim was evidently enjoying his sport as he continued to torment me; thrusting the broomstick towards my abdomen again… and again… and again, smirking as he did so.

Tears were running down my cheeks, but he was relishing every second of my torment. I knew that just a few inches more and my baby could have gone stone cold inside the womb. He eventually left me, still clutching the broom, as I sobbed uncontrollably beside the geese pen. I'm sure he was laughing.

My only escape valve was Jim's mother, his sister Alice Fay and her husband James. I visited Alice and James as much as I could to get away from Jim. I was very big now and Alice Fay, who had been through the trauma of childbirth herself, was very attentive towards me. She was lovely and we got on well.

I liked her husband too, but he couldn't understand a word I said. Alice Fay had to interpret for him. It was like I was speaking Swahili or something. You know, I'm convinced he thought I was speaking an alien tongue. To be fair, there were people in the south of England who were completely baffled by the North East dialect.

Despite our linguistic barriers, Jim's family thought I was all 'crumpets and tea', a proper little English rose. Please tell that to someone from Hampstead or Winchester, would you? They'd laugh you out of the room. Why they thought I spoke like 'crumpets and tea' is beyond me.

Imperceptibly - to me at least - I began to develop a southern drawl like my in-laws. Gradually, they found me a bit easier to understand, which was just as well because my line to Jim was growing fuzzier by the day. He understood me alright, but he was damned if he was going to listen.

When he was sober everything was just about alright. I was forever treading on eggshells and fearing the next slap, but in fact that never happened when he was off the booze. For this reason, I dreaded the Social Security cheque dropping through the letterbox, because it meant Jim would be straight out the door, squandering our money on cheap liqueur and up to God knows what.

Back in England, he seemed the perfect Southern gentleman, so I arrived in America expecting him to treat me like an English princess, but the booze turned him into a monster. He beat me like I was a pack mule; used me as his punchbag in cold, drunken rages.

The sober days were the most blessed relief and I always knew which ones these were because the benefits cheque had either not arrived or had run out. We would go to a drive-in movie or a restaurant and have a perfectly pleasant time. It was almost like the early days in Middlesbrough.

I wouldn't call him a gentleman when he was sober, but he wasn't such the ogre. He was alright with me - that's as far as it goes. But that was enough for me in the grand scheme of things.

In truth, I was frightened to death of him. I didn't know which way it would go from one day to the next. How long would this go on? It had already gone far beyond anything that could be put down to a temporary aberration or early-marriage jitters. This *was* Jim without question and there was plainly no other Jim, and therefore no hope of coaxing the marriage into anything remotely resembling a working partnership. Eventually, something terrible would surely happen to me or, God forbid, my child.

In the beginning, when we were at the Hotel Royal, I held on to the illusion that the beatings would eventually stop. I knew they wouldn't, but I wanted to believe that they would. After all, you don't stop loving them straight away, do you? It takes a while, but gradually they just kill all the love.

One night, Jim got his mum's old Chevy out and took me to watch a Bette Davis movie at the local drive-in. It was a thriller called 'Hush... Hush, Sweet Charlotte', and it scared the life out of me. Davis was brilliant, as usual, but her acting and facial expressions were so good she could put the fear of God in you. She played a Southern belle called Charlotte Hollis, who had been falsely accused of killing her lover, who had his head chopped off and his hand severed by a cleaver in the summerhouse on a plantation owned by her wealthy family in Louisiana. I looked over at Jim who seemed unperturbed by the horror on screen and had one hand resting on the steering wheel.

I was convinced the horror movie was a premonition of things to come. It scared the living daylights out of me, but I didn't dare show Jim how frightened I was because I knew he'd have played on it; turned my insides to jelly. It was a great movie, but I was too terrified to enjoy it. I couldn't wait to get back to the shack.

Jim's mother was scrupulously clean but keeping the shack tidy was a thankless task. It was crawling with rodents and cockroaches and the heat sometimes made the shack hum. It was so basic it would probably have been condemned back home.

Fanny's house didn't even have a TV when I arrived - only grandma had a television set. If there was anything worth watching, we'd crowd around her old black-and-white, but I don't remember watching much. I was too busy with the geese and Jim's hands.

It was the first time I'd ever heard of 'soap operas', which back then were just midday television dramas for housewives. They were called 'soaps' because the shows were sponsored by soap and detergent companies. The first one I ever saw was The Guiding Light. It was awful and terribly corny, but it ran from 1952 to 2009 - a Guinness world record! With little else to watch, I gorged on Captain Kangaroo, the kids' TV programme, which was shown on weekdays in the morning. I was also hooked on Secret Agent, the series with Patrick McGoohan as a secret-service agent. It was a brilliant series, watched by millions in the 1960s, but in England it was called Danger Man.

Apart from that, American TV back then was pretty naff, but Jim and his family seemed to lap it up. They'd be glued to the set and I'd be thinking: "What the hell?"

There was really nothing to do in this rural backwater and life in Mansfield was incredibly slow. You just went where your husband went.

When Jim's brother - the drunk who was barred from the town - came over, their idea of a day out was to go and see their dad's grave, which was near a memorial to the civil war out in the county somewhere.

They always looked forward to going into the shack shop out there, which sold saddles and things. It was just like the ones you'd see in the Westerns, with a porch out front. I don't remember seeing anything remotely interesting inside the shop, but I do remember the overpowering smell of leather and sweat.

Everything wilted and sweated out here because it was so damn hot. I had permanent beads of sweat on my top lip from the humidity and, being a natural red-head with fair skin, I suffered in the relentless, oppressive heat. I never wore shoes and always went barefoot. Rain was like a Godsend.

One day it pelted it down and I went outside to immerse myself in the soft, cooling raindrops. It was glorious, heaven-sent: I literally lapped up the rain, slurping it back with my tongue. They were all laughing at me. They found it hilarious, but the relief was such that I didn't care. Five minutes later, the rain had stopped and it was as if it had never been raining 'cos the heat just zapped all the moisture from air. It was way too hot for me out there and I couldn't cope with it. Jim just told me to get over it.

I sought solace in cigarettes and smoked like a chimney. I'd smoked since I was 15 - my father was a heavy smoker and I'd taken my cue from him, I suppose - but now I was gobbling them, easily smoking over 20 cigarettes a day. There was a garage just over the road from the shack where they sold Marlboros. I smoked nothing but Marlboros, the 'cowboy's cigarette'.

Whenever Jim was away on the pretext of looking for work - he was always "looking for work", usually in Galveston, Texas - I'd forge his signature on his Social Security cheque and hop straight over to the garage. There was no other way to get hold of any money to buy my cigarettes.

One day I walked over to the garage barefoot. I sloped down the grass at the front of the shack and trod on a slithering snake. I hadn't seen it until it was too late. It was probably just a grass snake, but I nearly jumped out of my skin. I must have leapt six feet in the air, shrieking like a banshee. I nearly died with shock, but I carried on regardless, and shoeless, because I was craving my cigs.

It was Jim's mother who taught me how to forge his signature, so I could get hold of some money. There was nothing else coming in, so I felt no guilt.

I wasn't eating much, apart from cigarettes. I was fed, I was looked after, but I didn't like the food. Black-eyed peas and yams were not my thing: I hated them. I like sweet potatoes now, but I couldn't stand them back then. And then there was the dreaded butter milk, from cartons: disgusting.

We'd sit around the old wooden table in the kitchen, with the patter of mice's feet above us in the rafters. Jim always devoured his food, which was prepared by the black maid who wasn't much of a cook as far as I could see. She'd even boil potatoes with fat in the water! It was greasy and horrible.

Jim's mother and I used to go to a supermarket down the highway and the only thing I recognised was Campbell's Condensed Chicken Soup – I lived on the stuff. I was pregnant, so I should have been eating for two, but I was losing weight even though I was with child. My weight plummeted alarmingly but my husband didn't seem to notice, and when he wasn't out on the razz with his brother, all he seemed to talk about was "Goddamn niggers" and getting the geese in. If this was Southern charm, it wasn't what they showed in the movies.

Chapter 6

A sharp knife is but a pipe dream

Between our house and Jim's grandmother's, there was a pathway, like a dirt track, where all the black people lived, out back, out of the way, bootlegging and brewing their own hooch - anything to get hold of a bit of money so they could eat.

Moonshine was everywhere; I think Jim drank it. Well, he'd drink anything, wouldn't he?

He referred to this small ghetto as the place where "all the niggers" lived.

There were no toilets in the town for the blacks: they had to go up an alleyway, but then they would get arrested for indecent exposure. They were just "Goddamn niggers" out here; they had no rights whatsoever, not even to pee in privacy.

This was Klan territory, though I never saw any white hoods or burning crosses. I'm sure there were all kinds of horrific things going on in the dead of night, but I never saw any of it 'cos it would get dark about 7 o'clock and I'd be in by then, unless we went to the drive-in.

The whites were plain rotten to the blacks, but Jim's mum was nice to the coloured maid. I never heard his mum say anything wrong about black people, but Jim and his brothers were all unashamed racists. I mean deeply, pathologically, racist, like it was like their life's mission to do down the "niggers".

You couldn't make a hair appointment, go to the doctor's or even visit the laundrette without coming up against this thing that The South called racial segregation. The first time I needed a hair cut in Louisiana, I didn't know where to go, so I looked in the Yellow Pages and found the number for a hair salon I'd seen while out shopping with Jim's mum, so I rang them to make an appointment. A woman answered the phone and I said I wanted to make an appointment for a few days hence.

"Yes'm, I don't think so," she said.

It was unmistakably a black woman.

I was knocked back. Why couldn't I make a hair appointment?

"Sorry ma'am," she says, "this is a coloured-ladies' hair salon."

They barred whites because they had to: they weren't allowed to cut white people's hair. It was total separation; like parallel worlds.

I got to know many coloured people in Mansfield and they were just people: perfectly nice, with their own flaws and of course their own worries, but nice as pie. Make no mistake, they were scared to death, and no wonder. They'd been worn down by years of persecution and had no real identity of their own. The astonishing thing for me was that they all seemed so happy despite the deprivations, the shambolic living conditions and the rampant injustice. They were well and truly under the thumb of the whites, and enduring daily humiliations was, for them, just a way of life.

Can you imagine what it's like to step out of your front door each morning and not know whether someone's going to spit on you or hurl vile racist abuse in your direction for no good reason; or, at worst, maybe lynch you or beat you to a pulp? How they ever managed to get by is beyond me.

I remember thinking how utterly disproportionate the difference was between the lives of the whites and those of the blacks in the south, yet how tiny the reason for that discrepancy: a simple differentiation of the pigment of one's skin. How utterly bizarre; how completely insane. And how horribly unjust.

There was a white lady who lived in a shack out back who had a young daughter in a wheelchair. The disabled daughter, who I think had polio, was the only one in town who understood my accent. She must have had some special kind of interpretive skills that no-one else in Mansfield possessed, 'cos whatever I said, and however crudely I intoned my Teesside accent, she got it. It was really weird 'cos she was the only one who could decipher the seemingly indecipherable.

One day we were sat out back having a coffee with her mother's black maid from Social Service. The maid had a little boy and I asked how old he was.

"Yes'm," she said.

That was "Yes ma'am", and that was how the black women addressed the white women over there.

"Yes'm, I don't know, Miss Valri," she said. "I knowd that he was born on a Shoosday, but yes'm, I don't know when."

The black maids called me Miss 'Valrie'. I told them just Valerie was okay, but they insisted on "Mz Valr-ee". Heaven knows what Jim would have made of it, but I don't think he truly understood just how close I was to them because he was always away, usually in Galveston with his brother, "looking for work".

I don't believe for one moment that he was looking for employment, but what I did know was that his brother had shacked up with an older lady out there who was loaded. The rich southern lady had a 15-year-old daughter who was by all accounts very nice-looking, tall and blonde.

One night, they came back to Louisiana in the middle of the night: there was Jim, his brother, the older rich lady and her teenage daughter. Jim threw me out of bed so the young girl could get in with him. And the girl's mother was there! Astonishingly, it didn't seem to bother her one jot.

I was almost fast asleep when they turned up. I thought I was seeing things at first: it was far too strange to be real. But I knew full well that my husband was deadly serious, and I crawled out of bed. They were all giggling and probably drunk. I ran, sobbing again, over to Jim's grandma's house, where Jim's uncle - Fanny's brother - was staying.

"It's alright, you can stay here," he said.

I slept in the back bedroom and shed buckets. The degradation was beyond anything a human being should have to tolerate. Being tossed out of bed by your own husband, to be replaced by a strange teenage girl, in the dead of night and without warning, was surely a first, even in this town.

I had absolutely no doubt that Jim had had his way with her - and all in the presence of her mother. How could she live with herself? And who *were* these people?

Afterwards, I got to thinking about the bullet wound I had spotted near Jim's groin. I could only assume that he'd been shot by someone's husband.

I was starting to think about killing the bastard myself. I mean, it had got to the stage where it was either me or him.

There are so many wives who, in my situation, would have reached for the knife and stabbed him in his sleep, long before I was even thinking about it, but for some reason I persevered with this hopeless and pointless marriage. I thought about it, believe me - many, many times.

I'd be laid in bed as Jim slept off the booze, snoring so loudly it almost made the bed shake, and what had previously seemed unthinkable was now entering my head on a frighteningly-regular basis.

So many nights spent thinking deep, dark thoughts into the early hours, not just about my absurd and increasingly-dangerous situation, but how I might go about getting rid of this knave of a husband. Knives entered my mind: knives and a quick thrust towards the heart, slicing right through that inert, booze-addled body.

I'd stare up at the ceiling crawling with cockroaches and think: "If I go into the kitchen now and get a knife, I could stab him."

And no-one could stop me 'cos everyone was fast asleep and, surely, I'd be doing everyone a favour? Even his mother. Yes, she'd thank me, surely?

It makes me shudder now, but I played out that scene in my mind so many times: creeping out of bed in the middle of the night, tip-toeing into the kitchen in my nightie, quietly opening the wooden drawer; then clasping the razor-sharp blade between my fingers and turning on my heels; back to the bedroom, where I creak the door open and ease it ever so gently back into its slot. I slide over to the side of the bed where Jim is still snoring, the glint of the blade illuminating his oblivious, drunken face. Then I crouch down, one knee resting on the edge of the bed, and plunge the serrated blade into his heart and stomach. He wakes momentarily and lets out a cry, but his heart gives out, he gasps, and then he's gone. I run away into the night.

These were no pipe dreams; these were fully-conscious, serious thoughts, right up to the point where I was about to get out of bed and slide over to the kitchen. The only reason that knife never entered my hand and pierced Jim's ruddy flesh was because, despite my desperation, and despite teetering on the edge of an emotional breakdown, I was too sensible to go ahead with it. I knew what the consequences would be and was fully aware how the confederate states dealt with "deranged" wives who turn the knife on their husbands. Better to be a battered wife than in some rotten, putrid, Dixie jail, eating gruel and slopping out in the morning. I realised that at some point I'd have to untangle myself from this mess, one way or another, and the chances of doing that while banged up in some fetid, hell-hole penitentiary would make my chances even slimmer than they were now. I didn't want Johnny Cash singing about me in some strangled ballad 20 years down the line. I could just imagine him rhapsodising about James Olan Bumbard "gunning that bad bitch down" after a barrel-full of beer.

In reality, Jim - who seemed blessed with more than his fair share of luck - would've caught the shimmer of the kitchen knife, woken up and given me a heavy beating, maybe even turned the knife on me. If it was me who got sliced up, then at least I'd be out of this horror and away from him. One of us would have to go sooner or later: it just seemed inevitable.

Despite all my hope and endless optimism (still desperately seeking the husband I thought I knew in Middlesbrough, maybe?), I now knew, once and for all, that that man never existed. Jim was no good, period. And how ironic were those initials of his: J.O.B - the one thing he never held down, unlike his liqueur.

I knew after the incident with the girl in our bed that I'd have to get out of there somehow, otherwise I'd surely slip into mental infirmity (if I survived at all).

Who knows? I might even turn into one of the hillbilly bunch: a green-eyed, scar-faced old harridan reeking of goose liver and sweeping the porch of a morning, while my husband sleeps off another whisky binge.

To be kicked out of one's bed by one's own husband to make way for a girl who wore pigtails - and all in front of her mother - was as degrading and humiliating an experience as one could imagine. And all while I was pregnant and had no money and was getting bigger by the day. I needed clothes for bigger-sized ladies, but there was no money to buy them. The little we had went on food and Jim's constant thirst.

One night, we went to visit some of Jim's friends and I couldn't wait to get out of there. It was a bunch of men and women drinking and playing cards all night. I felt very uncomfortable and I think the only reason Jim took me was because his bawdy friends were curious about the English wife he had brought home.

Bored out of my mind, I flicked through the pages of a catalogue which belonged to the female host. Jim allowed me to order some maternity dresses out of the index, but the dresses never materialised because he cancelled them the following day. Clearly, he had no intention of buying them for me.

Then inspiration struck when I was round at Jim's sister's house at the other end of the highway. Alice-Fay used to get chicken feed delivered in light-coloured sacks and I thought I might be able to use the material from the feed sacks to make maternity dresses.

I asked Alice Fay if I could take a few sacks and she gave me half a dozen. I got Jim's mum's old treadle machine out, the ones with the pedal, except this one looked about 400 years old. I had to wash the feed sacks first, very thoroughly because they were stained and reeked to high heaven. I'd never sewn in my life except at school, but I sat down and just did it.

I was a lousy sewer at school, but I was always very resourceful when push came to shove and right now I needed maternity clothes because I was poking out at all angles. I was dead proud of my new chicken-feed-sack clothes. In fact, I was over the moon.

His mother got us an apartment (if that's what you'd call it) somewhere out in Mansfield. It was a plain, tiny old thing in the back garden of this woman's house. It was, nominally at least, a self-contained flat, but, if truth be told, more of a one-bedroom bungalow on a tiny scale: dilapidated, depressed and, quite frankly, ugly. Surely a metaphor for our marriage.

I suppose Fanny, God bless her, realised we'd have to have our independence eventually, but at what cost, heaven knows.

She knew the lady who owned the house and asked her if she could accommodate her son and his wife. The owner was an agreeable lady and said we could move in straight away, although there might be a few minor "adjustments" needed - not least a liberal application of pesticide. As it turned out, the place was riddled with cockroaches. Me and Jim's mum went in one day to give it a thorough clean before we moved in because the place was alive with the things.

Jim's mum scrubbed the place clean. We just cleaned everything, top to bottom, and it took us virtually a whole day.

We moved in the next day and I went into the kitchen to get some cereal from the cupboard. I reached in to get some cornflakes and these huge cockroaches were crawling all over my arm. They used to crack when you stood on them. These things have been with us for 320 million years: they even outlasted the dinosaurs. In Louisiana, they were in every nook and cranny. When you were in the shower, they marched towards you like an army, in formation. Every time I took my dressing gown off the back of the door, I'd have to shake it and all the cockroaches would tumble to the floor, then march off in serried ranks.

We didn't last long at the apartment - precisely two weeks - because Jim buggered off again and didn't pay the rent. His mum paid the first week's rent for us because she knew he wasn't handing any money over to the landlady, but then we got turfed out and I had to go back to the shack and purgatory.

I think Jim had stayed at the 'apartment' just one night and then went off to Galveston or wherever. I can only remember being there on my own. Just me and the cockroaches.

And then I got word that my father was coming over to America on business. To Ohio, to be precise, but I sensed salvation.

Chapter 7

The Flight

My father was planning to visit us at the shack during his business trip to the States. I counted down the days to his arrival with a desperation bordering on mania.

I'd never written home about anything that happened in Mansfield because I didn't want to worry my parents, and I suppose I wanted to be spared the shame of admitting that I'd made a terrible, life-altering mistake.

Yet the more I thought about it, maybe it wasn't such a good idea that my father, the businessman, came to red-neck county and our tiny shack with his suit on and briefcase in hand. It had never occurred to me until now that my father would be appalled at these squalid living conditions because, worryingly, I had got used to the way we lived, and to me it had become the norm.

Dad's flight was just days away when I turned round to Fanny in the kitchen and said: "I can't have my father coming here when Jim's like he is. I can't do it."

The expression on her face was one I shall never forget. She looked as if she was about to reveal some deep, dark secret.

Looking straight into my eyes with pools of sadness and a profound despair, she said: "I think there's something that you ought to know. Let's drive to Alice Faye's and we can all sit down. We'll tell you everything."

An icy chill ran down my spine because I knew in my heart that it had to be something about Jim and it couldn't be good. But what could possibly be worse than I had seen already?

We drove down to Alice Fay's and they sat me down; made a pot of coffee. They told me Jim already had five wives with no divorces - and they all had children to him. He'd married one of them, a Texan woman, just 15 months before he got hitched to me. It hit me like a bombshell. How could I have been so naïve?

Five times he'd been 'down the aisle' (or most probably just a backwater registry office), and I didn't know a damn thing about it.

Fanny and Alice Fay looked at me with great pity, so sad were they for me and my hopeless situation.

Fanny said every time the wives got pregnant he beat them and brought them to her. She said they were all sluts whom Jim had bedded but then left after they had borne him children.

"We saw you and we couldn't believe it, because you were obviously a nice girl from a nice family and we didn't know what to do with you," she said.

"And you weren't eating properly, and you were losing weight, and we thought you might miscarry, so we didn't say anything about the wives."

She said that before they met me, they had assumed I was just another one of Jim's floozies. Or, as Fanny put it at the time: "Oh, here's another slut."

According to his mum, Jim never hit a woman until she was pregnant. I instinctively felt my bump and went cold: now it all made sense.

It seemed that Jim had something against pregnancies, and most certainly against the women who got pregnant. Clearly, he didn't want them or the kids: he just wanted to shag.

I think he must have thought: "God, I'm not having any of this; it's too much like family life."

Fanny's revelations knocked me for six - he'd been whoring around even before I got there!

And then it all came back to me in a stream of dire consciousness: the gunshot wound to the groin, the trips out to Galveston to "look for work", the girl in the bed, my intuition regarding Jim's disposition towards my best mate Kathy, the rumours about rich women that coincided with Jim's many sojourns in Texas with his brother.

Five wives in different states – good work Jimbo! He'd obviously been a busy boy for one so idle, or maybe he just liked wedding cake.

I'd become accustomed to Jim's drinking, his brutishness, his warped, racist bigotry, but I'll be honest, I never had him down as a bigamist (or, more precisely, a polygamist). Of course, I always suspected womanising and whoring, but not marriage on such an epic scale. His life's goal was pretty clear: meet a woman, marry her, get her pregnant, then ditch her. He was white-trash hillbilly to the core. The epitome.

And then I thought back to Hartlepool and that large, framed picture of himself that he had brought from the States when he was working on the rigs. It sounds crazy, but I'd never given it a second thought at the time. Oh, stupid, stupid me. He must have given it to all his wives; that's why the name looked scratched out.

It was only now, after Fanny's bombshell, that I realised the insanity of the trust that I had placed in him. I was obviously blinded by love, but now I think: "Why the hell would he want to bring that picture over with him?"

And give it to a British woman who would fall for him. Again, stupid, gullible me.

Polygamy was a federal offence in the States under what was known as the Edmunds Act, and there were laws against taking more than one wife in all 50 states. But Jim, the crafty old fox, had got around this by going from one state to the next, impregnating girls and then shooting over county lines, leaving them to bring up the child on their own, probably penniless and destitute and begging for help from the state.

He knew that as long as he didn't marry more than one girl in any given state he was home and dry, because the police in one state didn't interfere with the police in another state.

I thought about those girls and it made me shudder. Hustlers or not, they were women. How many had he duffed up like he did me? How many had he slapped around after a night on the booze, then left in the gutter? I ached for these girls like I ached for myself.

I thought how easy it must have been for Jim to lure me into his trap. This was his practice; this was his game; honed over the years, to the point where it's practically second nature. An effortless exercise in deceit, you might say.

He'd steamrollered through the lives of at least six young women, leaving behind a wreckage. I wondered what their lives must be now. Were they still alive? Who shot him? One of them or a jealous ex-husband?

This is a man who sailed through a statute signed into law in 1882 with nary a mark on him. Really, what chance did we have? I assumed the others must have been ready for the plucking too. He obviously knew how to pick 'em. We were easy prey.

I have to hand it to Jim: he was the perfect liar, a master of his art. He had me fooled alright.

And not just the perfect liar, but a compulsive one, of the sort that actually believe the lie themselves. You may have your suspicions, even cast-iron proof, but if you raise them, you just get blank stares and honeyed words to throw you off the scent and allay your fears. But a deception on Jim's scale cannot last forever: the crimes are so egregious and the trail of victims so long that it's bound to catch up with them in the end. Of course, by then the damage is done: so many shattered lives, too many young women with fatherless children. I've got one on the way.

We went back to Fanny's house and I wrote an 18-page letter to my parents telling them everything. Jim was away in Galveston again, so I grabbed a pen from the small bureau in the bedroom and just poured my heart out as tears blotted the white stationery. It was an unfiltered account of my torment from the moment I touched down on the Gulf of Mexico. I spared no detail: this was final, and I wanted my parents to know that I had nowhere to hide, that I was on the brink.

Emotions that had been bubbling away inside of me for six long months seemed all the more horrific for being jotted down in black ink: the incessant beatings, the fear, the humiliations, the entire grand hoax from beginning to end.

There was no longer any point in hiding it: Fanny's revelations had made the situation intractable. There was no option but to flee.

Right from the very beginning, right back to the Grand Hotel when Jim had whisked me off my feet, he thought of me as nothing more than a slut who could be bedded, used, milked and then discarded like an old rag, a chicken-feed sack, a common hussy.

How could I have been so gullible? I prided myself on my perceptiveness, my intuition, my savviness and common sense. I always thought my feminine wiles would shield me from the cads and the charlatans, but of course I was just another patsy, a sucker for Jim's southern affectations and, let's be honest, his animal magnetism. When it came to sheer fox-like cunning and outrageous deceit, Jim was plainly in a league of his own. I'd been had, duped, hoaxed, by a master manipulator. Clearly, I was out of my depth.

I sent the letter by air-mail - special delivery - to Middlesbrough, worrying it might give father a cardiac arrest. I imagined their shock as they opened the envelope and read the first few lines. My father's furrowed brow, followed by disbelief, then anger; mother in the background shaking her head and saying what a stupid, naïve little bitch I had been. Probably just confirmation, should she need it, that I was a mistake at birth. I imagined father tossing the letter into the coal fire and muttering all kinds of profanities. But, honestly, I think they were both genuinely upset about the whole business, in their own, queer way.

I knew that, despite the anger and the confusion, father's overriding concern would be for my safety and my escape. He'd get me out of here, for sure.

For the next 48 hours, I waited on tenterhooks for the phone to ring. Every time we got a phone call my heart would jump and my throat would go dry. I longed to hear my father's soothing, reassuring voice. I was desperate for him to get here before the return of Jim.

Two long days had passed since I'd sent the letter and then, one morning, the black maid at Jim's grandma's shouted: "Mz Valr-ee... telephooone."

Jim's grandma was the only one in the family to have a phone, thank God. I knew who it would be and legged it up to grandma's, with Jim's mum shouting behind me: "Be careful, you're pregnant!"

I burst into the shack, lungs heaving, cheeks burning, and the black maid passed me the telephone. I grasped the old handset and waited for his voice to filter down the wires. I was so out of breath I don't remember saying anything at all.

"Can you meet me at the airport at Shreveport at 11 o'clock tomorrow night?" said father.

And I felt this big weight lift off my shoulders. Apparently, dad's flight had been booked a few days in advance for the business trip, but he'd gone to the travel agents in Middlesbrough after receiving my letter and said he needed an earlier flight.

"When for?" said the agent.

"Yesterday," he said.

The flight was booked. He came straight over. Oh, please Lord, let him get here before Jim gets back.

I got the call that he was at the airport and I got this couple who knew Jim's mum to drive me and his mother to the airport in Shreveport 'cos I didn't think his mother's old Chevy would have made it. It would not be unfair to say that Fanny's vehicle wouldn't have looked out of place in the Ant Hill Mob.

Shreveport was about 40 miles away, but it seemed to take an age. I got out of the car, ran up to the terminal and waited. I saw this typically English-looking man wearing a Trilby hat get off the plane and my heart just leapt with joy and relief. It was the best sight I'd ever seen.

My emotions were running so high it all seems like a blur now and I can't remember what I said to him, nor he to me. I must have run into his arms and hugged him like the great liberator. I must have said, "Oh dad, thank God", but I don't remember.

There were definitely tears, a big hug; that's all I remember other than walking through the airport back to the car and this Louisiana couple who had quite possibly saved my life.

We drove down the highway back to Mansfield. As we approached the county limits, there was this big sign which read: 'Welcome to DeSoto County'.

DeSoto County was in neighbouring Mississippi and Mansfield was in DeSoto parish, Louisiana, which was a bit odd. I looked over at my father who was staring quizzically at this sign. 'DeSoto' was clearly beyond his linguistic grasp.

"De-sow-tow… De-sow-tow," he said to himself.

"De…sor…tor," he repeated in his thick Teesside accent. Everybody in the car was howling. In Lousiana, they pronounced it 'DeSoooda'. A bit like 'disorder' – how fitting.

We arrived back in Mansfield and my blood froze. Was he back? I had no idea. I prayed to God that he wasn't.

We got out of the car and the couple drove off, giving us a friendly wave and wishing us luck. What lovely people. God bless them.

Me and dad walked up the grass slope to the shack and I remember being racked with fear that Jim would be sleeping off a drink in the bedroom. Who knows, he might even open the door to us with that big, broad, wolf-like grin knowing the bastard. Mercifully, the house was empty.

Fanny went and stayed at grandma's house next-door so me and dad could stay in the house on our own and talk about stuff.

We sat down on the tatty old settee in the front room. My father grimaced, looked around the shack with something approaching shock and horror, and said: "How have you been living like this?"

He was gobsmacked, but to me it was home. I'd got used to it, so I was somewhat taken aback. It was very basic, but it was clean.

Father was appalled: he couldn't believe I'd been slumming it all these months. That night, he slept with his passport and his wallet under his pillow. And one night was all he could bear.

The next day was the 4th of July - American Independence Day. We were sat on the front porch eating water melon with the family, celebrating the anniversary. Water melon was probably all they could afford.

Jim, mercifully, hadn't shown up yet. He'd disappeared for weeks, to Galveston again, with his brother. I suppose they were living off that rich old woman, she with the teenage sacrificial lamb who had slept in my bed, but frankly I couldn't be sure what they'd been up to.

Later that day, when all the water melon had run out, we left. Independence Day indeed.

Dad joked that it was "the second time they had thrown the British out", but at the time it didn't seem funny.

I got my stuff together in the front bedroom, terrified that Jim would turn up at the last moment. I packed my bags frantically and gave Fanny a big hug. More tears: I felt like I was deserting her. She told me to take care of myself and looked down pensively at my baby bump.

I think the same guy took us back to the airport, and me and my father flew out to Atlanta. We stayed overnight in a hotel.

The next day, father flew out to Ohio on business and I got a plane to Heathrow, vomiting all the way over the Atlantic. Not because of the enormity of what I had just done, or from what I was fleeing, but because I was six-months pregnant and the toll on my health had been too heavy a burden for me to carry, and of course there had been no medical attention.

As we crossed the ocean, I looked out of my window seat across this vast blue expanse and it hit me like a thunderbolt: I'd been set up from word go. The entrapment at The Grand hotel, the charm, the "Thank you ma'ams"; my suspicions regarding Jim and Kathy (of course, I was right all along); the drunken ambivalence at the airport; the beatings; the broomstick; the girl in the bed, the five wives; and, most of all, the distinct lack of affection, or rather the complete lack of any sort of marital obligation.

He'd felt nothing for me from the outset: that was perfectly clear now. I'd been had, but worse: I'd been a willing accomplice in my own downfall. And the man who had sunk me was a semi-literate, red-neck hillbilly, an interstate whore master who had impregnated women (God knows how many) with impunity.

My utter naivete gnawed me to the bone. Surely to commit oneself to some dystopian hick hell, and all perfectly willingly, and from a comfortable middle-class background, was sheer insanity?

It's very strange, I know, but you don't stop loving someone straight away when they beat you. How could you? The alteration is too fast. You loved that person, so when, the next day, he sticks his fist into your face, does that love go away? No, it doesn't. It's impossible.

The one part I missed out on, thankfully, was being killed, as I assumed I must surely have been in the long-run, however long the run may have lasted. The realisation that I would surely have been left dead, delirious or destitute chilled me to the bone – but why only now? On this plane? Had I been brainwashed by this hoodlum?

And what the hell did I think I was going to do with a six-month visa once it had expired? Maybe I could have stayed on because I was married to a US citizen, but who knows? Oh, so naïve, and so loving and willing.

I went for love and got zilch. I was blinded. I lived in a shack, swatted insects and saw at first hand the terrible plight of "the negroes". But other than that, I spent half a year doing nothing apart from eating bad food, getting slapped around, ushering geese into pens and practising to perfection the fraudulent signing of Social Service cheques. Oh, and learning how to speak with a southern drawl, so at least people could understand me.

I landed at Heathrow and immediately felt I was on home ground - an ecstatic relief. I immediately rang mother. Apparently, she'd been beside herself with worry. How bizarre.

I'd heard somebody had given her a sleeping tablet 'cos she was in such a state of anxiety after receiving my letter. She'd been worried to death about getting me home. How very, very strange, and how utterly unpredictable life is. Maybe the bitch had a caring side after all - or a scintilla, at least.

I was ringing and ringing and ringing, but there was no answer. Finally, there was a click on the other end and I heard mother's voice. Not soft or reassuring by any means, but, right now, deliverance. I felt my heart lift.

"Hello marmmy, this is Valrie," I said in a strange, southern-American accent.

She didn't know who the hell it was: my Dixie drawl had her totally baffled, and she'd just woken up after swallowing a sleeping tablet. As she came around, it became clear that the little Dixie chick on the other end of the line was indeed her long-lost daughter, but not quite the one who had left her behind six months earlier.

I told her I was flying from Heathrow to Teesside and I'd be there at such and such a time. She said she'd drive out to meet me when we touched down.

When I stepped out of the cabin and onto the air-stair, the first thing that hit me was the freshness of the air and the lack of humidity. I took my first step back on English soil and was overcome by emotion. The tears were just gushing out of me – and I hadn't even seen mother yet.

She was waiting for me in the terminal, looking uncharacteristically distressed, relieved, saddened and joyful all at the same time. She was crying – unbelievable! Yes, sobbing her eyes out.

It was the first time I'd seen even the tiniest hint of emotion from what I assumed to be an unflappable soul. She even gave me a hug – that in itself was a first.

We drove back to my parents' bungalow in Brookfield, both of us in floods of tears. I told her, in precis, what had happened over the past six months and noticed she was holding the steering wheel very tightly. Her eyes were sodden.

I look back now and think there must have been another side to her. After all, there's always another side to everyone. And maybe, looking back, she just never let this other side surface. But why? And what was stopping her from showing emotion, particularly towards her only child?

If her tears at the airport revealed a caring side and a natural maternal instinct, why bury it under a thick layer of steel? What was the reason? Was she hiding something? The simple fact is that she probably did have a caring side but, for whatever reason, she couldn't show it.

The first thought that struck me as we rolled into the driveway in father's big Ford Corsair was how splendid the bungalow looked in the glistening summer sun. Compared to the shack, it was a palace.

I suddenly felt a pang of nostalgia for times past. Just the thought of the sanctity of my own four walls, in the back bedroom, and my mother's heavy hands became a distant memory. After the beatings dished out by Jim, mother's assaults faded into obscurity.

We crossed the threshold like a genuine mother and daughter and sat down for a cup of tea. The conversation turned immediately to Mansfield and the goings-on inside the shack that had been my home for half a year.

Mother made a nice supper and we sat down at the kitchen table where we talked well into the night, liked we'd never talked before. It was women's talk, the like of which I'd never had with her. And she listened, avidly, with empathy and even sympathy. Her mouth dropped, and my heart strained, as I recounted every last detail of my life as Mrs James Olan Bumbard. She, too, realised she'd been had.

The food was Manna from heaven and I ate ravenously. Whatever else you might think about my mother, she was a damn good cook: rabbit pies, Sunday dinners, nice thick soups, mash potato and gravy. And her stews were just divine: she used to boil the bones so the meat would slowly come away, adding to the tenderness.

In an instant, black-eyed peas and butter milk just vanished from memory. All this bourgeois décor and the sheer cleanliness of the place (not a cockroach in sight) made the shack in Mansfield look positively Medieval.

Jim and the hut were suddenly long gone. There was an ocean and thousands of miles between us at last, yet his child was right here inside me, nestling inside my womb like a mischievous imp. I immediately hated the child: how could I not?

After all, how would he or she turn out? Just like him? Undoubtedly, in my mind, the answer was yes. I was convinced Jim would continue to haunt me by proxy. I was certain I was carrying Jim Mark II and that it would be a boy and look just like him.

I must get rid of this thing growing inside me or kill myself. And most certainly, I hope Jim dies.

Chapter 8

Goodbye Little One

I ate like a pig when I came home; never stopped. Great dollops of mash potato; mother's great steaming stews with big, fat dumplings; all devoured with hungry relish. I gorged on corned beef, fish and chips, and proper vegetables. She also made a great rabbit pie.

I started putting weight back on and I was feeling a bit more like my old self, but not quite. I was scarred for sure and I knew the road would be a long one.

I gobbled cigarettes with even greater relish than I did my food. I was going through two packs a day to help me cope with the stress.

The baby was about due, but lots of mothers smoked back then. Just thinking about giving birth to a little Jim sent me into paroxysms of fear and anxiety. I was trying to heal, but everywhere I went, his child came with me and the ghost of Jim stalked me at every turn.

I was convinced it would be a boy and look just like him, and if that were the case there was no way I could bring up that child and love that child.

I was walking home from the fish shop one night when I decided the baby would have to be adopted. I told my parents and they said that whatever I decided to do, they would stand by me. They said I could keep the baby in the bungalow if I wanted, but I said I didn't think that was a good idea. I wanted to start afresh and that didn't include rearing son of Jim.

"Okay then," said my dad, who was back from the States.

"Whatever you do, we'll stick by you."

I hated this child that was growing inside me. It sounds a pretty rotten thing to say, but I have always believed in honesty and why should I mask my true feelings? I wanted rid; there's no two ways about it. Even mother couldn't understand my apparent

64

heartlessness, and she gave out every appearance of a woman with a heart of stone.

"Don't you feel anything when it kicks?" she said.

"No," I replied, "I wish it was dead. I wish I could fall down the stairs and lose it."

If proof were needed that I was carrying the son of Satan, I went into a labour from hell, in the hospital from hell. I was admitted to Parkside Maternity Hospital in Middlesbrough, a stain on the public health service. Ordinarily, I wouldn't have gone in there to have my toenails cut, but I needed this baby out and gone from my life and it was the nearest infirmary to our house. As bad luck would have it, the two surgeons who were supposed to perform the Caesarean were on holiday and I went into labour for five days and nights. It was horrendous.

The pain was so unbearable I just wanted to die. The physical trauma was bad enough, but the excruciating labour sent me bananas and I wanted them to put me in a dustbin because of how stupid I had been.

In my scrambled, dysfunctional brain, the thought kept popping into my head: "If they put me in a dustbin, I'll be rubbish and I won't hurt."

My father came to see my every day, but mother never showed up, even though he told her that "my Val's face is contorted in pain". I have not known pain like it before or since: there wasn't room for the baby to come out.

In the end, they yanked her out and ripped me to bits. And then my stitches got infected, so I had to stay in longer. It was a never-ending nightmare.

It was a girl - a little red-head like me. My double. She even had my thumbs. No little Jim after all, but there was no way I could keep her: she still had his genes and I'd still be a single mother.

My brow was drenched with sweat and I was laid out in bed, practically comatose and still reeling from the pain. They took the baby away 'cos I'd told them: "I don't want to see her; I don't want to touch her."

I never held her after the birth because I knew she'd have to be fostered straight away. Social Services were informed and a couple from Grangetown, a township near Middlesbrough, expressed an interest in fostering her. People from Social Services came to the hospital one day when mother finally made an appearance. They took the baby away to its fosterers in Grangetown.

Before they arrived, the sister at the hospital said: "I would like you to do something for me. I would like you to feed her and bathe her."

It was supposed to be part of the bonding ritual, but I wanted nothing to do with it.

"I know how you feel," she said.

"You have no idea how I feel at all," I replied.

She said: "You need to know that if you feed and clothe her, you can still part with her."

So I bathed and fed her - and I sobbed my eyes out. The poor thing was ringing wet from my tears.

Even my mother was crying, but I was determined that my heart wouldn't overrule my head. I'd been through too much. I'd made my mind up: the baby must go.

I'd even given her my Christian name, Hazel, but it was up to the adoptive parents if they wanted to change it.

I wanted a new life and that didn't include this baby. I knew that if I wanted a fresh start, the child could have no part in my life. There was just no way.

It was all a bit fuzzy, what with the painkillers and the emotion and the agonising pain. I think I just handed the baby over to the sister and she handed the girl over to the social workers in another room.

They kept me in hospital for ten days while they sorted out the infection. While I was laid up, the nurses brought in a bunch of flowers which had been sent by an old friend. My old flame Bill had clearly not forgotten about me. Even when I was in America, married, he must have been thinking about me.

I finally got home and sunk into a deep depression. I couldn't function, which was completely alien to a woman like me. I just sat and ate and thought and thought: deep, dark introspections which kept me awake all night and crumpled my sheets. I was consumed by fear and revulsion, for the mistakes I had made; for the baby I was about to give up for adoption; for the utter bloody mess I had made of my life; for the future; for everyone I felt I had let down, including myself.

I contemplated suicide, but only briefly: I was just too clever and sensible to go through with it. I realised, after a time, that I once had a life out there, in the US, which was plainly miserable, but now I had the chance of a new life over here. I even had a new name: Val. It was nice to have a new identity after six months as 'Valrie' the human punch bag.

I was, momentarily, on the brink of ending it all, but then I thought: "The bastard's not going to ruin my life anymore."

English stoicism, I suppose. That stiff upper lip, or maybe northern pig-headedness. It saw me through at the point of no return.

It wasn't the first time I'd embraced death as a better alternative to life. I'd contemplated suicide once before, when I was pregnant. It could have been the hormones going haywire; it could have been Jim; it could have been because I'd made a pig's ear of my young life; but there was no doubt I saw death, at least fleetingly, as an easy escape route from my troubles.

My decision to pull back and choose life had nothing to do with the baby. I wanted it to die during pregnancy. I was convinced it would be his double; never thought for a moment it would be a girl that looked just like me.

My father wrote to the hospital to complain about the missing surgeons which led to my excruciating labour in the absence of a C-section. He was seething; infuriated that because two blokes had decided to bugger off abroad, his daughter ended up in agony.

The only willing adoption society anywhere near us was in York. No other society would have her because there was no father's signature, so she was like a bastard in the eyes of the law.

We made two trips to York so they could interview me and find out more about my background. It was a hundred-mile round journey. Father went with me both times and we put Hazel in a carry cot on the back seat.

They asked me everything from my religion to the natural colour of my hair, which was ruby red and always had been since I was four, when I went from being bald to wispy red curls.

It really was like the Spanish Inquisition, but they've got to do it because they need to know every last detail about where the baby has come from and what sort of child she is likely to become, so they have a better idea of how well-suited the child is to the adoptive parents, and vice-versa.

In turn, they tell you stuff about the adopters except the finer details such as their names and addresses, which must remain confidential. All I knew was that they had been married 14 years; that the woman had red hair and that they would have to wait another 18 months after Hazel's adoption before they could adopt another child. Apparently, they also wanted a boy.

My daughter's upbringing, to this day, would remain a mystery to me. I just hoped she would never ask how she came into this world, because how could you explain Jim and Louisiana? Better to be blissfully unaware than face the grim truth.

On the second trip up to York, father stopped off at his shop 'cos my mother was working there. He wanted to show her the baby. It broke her heart and she bawled her eyes out. What a strange, complex woman. Or was it just a guilty conscience?

After I got back from the States, this hard-faced woman who abused me as a child was so afflicted by anxiety and fear for my safety that when she was alone in the house she kept my father's double-barrel shotgun near the front door in case Jim returned. I knew he wouldn't, but father's hunting rifle was always beside the door. She was petrified.

The last time we went up to the adoption society in York, father was in hospital with heart problems, so my uncle Ronnie took me. We had to pick up all of Hazel's stuff from the foster parents who'd bagged up her belongings and put them in a box. We had to have three of everything ready for the adoption centre: three nighties, three nappies, three sets of clothes, that sort of thing.

On the way up, Hazel filled her nappy and I didn't know how to change it. I made it up on the spot, just like I'd done with the chicken-feed sacks I'd made into maternity clothes in Mansfield. They were proper nappies in those days, not like the flimsy pieces of polymer you have today, and I had her cleaned and wrapped in no time.

She was asleep on the way up and when we arrived at the Adoption Society I picked her up in my arms and took her into the interview room. I sat her on my lap as these Adoption Society officials grilled me like I was on trial for some egregious crime. The adoption couple were sat in the next room.

68

This woman from the Adoption Society walked in, wrenched Hazel from my arms and said: "Thank you".

"Just a minute," I said, and gave my daughter a kiss. And then she was gone.

In the next room I could hear someone say: "Oh my God, she's beautiful!"

I choked up, but then I thought: "Oh, that's lovely, she's got a home."

There were no regrets: I wanted shot of her. I was just upset about the way the lady from the Adoption Society had taken her off me. She didn't give me a chance to say goodbye and she more or less snatched her off me.

I suppose that's the way they had to do it in case you had a change of heart at the last minute. It was quite dramatic, I must say.

I imagine they'd been trained that way, so you don't end up in a ridiculous tug 'o' war with the baby in the middle. Could there be anything more absurd and undignified, never mind gut-wrenchingly awful?

I remember saying to uncle Ronnie after I finally gave her up: "The first pub, I need a large whisky please."

On the way back, baby now gone, we went into the first pub we saw and had a large whisky apiece. There were more tears.

I felt this unbearable weight on my shoulders which even the finest malt whisky couldn't lift. It was the lowest of all lows.

Me, age six, feeding a feathered friend at Trafalgar square during the Festival of Britain, Summer 1951.

Date with the devil: My wedding to Jim, Middlesbrough Registry Office, January 1966. Jim seems innocent enough in this picture, and mother (right) appears to be uncharacteristically affectionate. I can assure you she was not.

Me with Kirkdale, my father's retriever, at my parents' bungalow in Scruton, North Yorks, 1969. Kirkdale was such a lovely dog but they got rid of him when he was about 10 and still full of health.

Me in the 1970s when I still had curly, ruby-red hair. I lost my red locks when Bill had a heart attack years later.

Bill and I getting married at Guisborough Registry Office, April 1968.

My baptism at the Oakwood Centre, Eaglescliffe, 2002. Jed and Victoria are about to submerge me in the cross-shaped pool.

Giving health-and-safety training to staff and volunteers at Jubilee Church, 2017.

Together in faith: Me, Bill and Victoria, October 2018.

Chapter 9

The Scarlet Woman

When I was pregnant with Hazel, I'd been to see Bill's mam whom I'd always kept in touch with. Bill took me out in his car for a run-out and we were just so incredibly comfortable together. It was that kind of relationship, where you're comfortable in silence.

It was obvious he still liked me, but he was more like a brother. I wasn't ready for a relationship after what happened in Hicksville. The scars would take years to heal and my emotions were still raw.

And then one day a letter drops into the hallway and it's marked 'United States of America'. Surely, it can't be him? It was.

Mother got hold of it and starts opening the envelope.

"Send it back; I don't want to know," I said.

"But he might say something that incriminates him, so we best open it," she said.

Mother steamed the envelope open and ran her eyes along the straggly handwriting. She handed me the letter.

I read the opening paragraph and that was enough: 'Oh honey, I couldn't believe it when I came home and you weren't there, and you'd gone without me.'

I put it back in the envelope and wrote, 'Return to sender'.

Jim was clearly trying to revert to charm again; the old Jim that had vanished within seconds of him meeting me at the airport in New Orleans.

And then my father told me things that I could scarcely believe, even knowing Jim as I did. He said that when we were saying our wedding vows at the registry office in Middlesbrough, he noticed Jim was smirking. He said he was fairly certain it was a smirk and not a smile, and I had no reason to doubt him. It explained a lot.

Father said that on the morning of the wedding, he and Jim had a glass of whisky together and maybe the drink had brought Jim's guard down for a second. With the marriage sanctified, Jim had allowed himself a sly chuckle: he'd bagged his sixth wife (allegedly and according to his mother), which I suppose is an achievement of sorts. My father said he wanted to punch him on the spot and knock the smirk off his face.

Now I think about it, I do remember Jim being unusually smiley that day, but I just assumed it was because he'd had too much whisky and was marrying his true love.

Just as I'm digesting this little nugget of information about my saintly husband, my father tells me there's one other thing I should know. That cheque that Jim had sent him for my flight to America, it had bounced. My mum and dad didn't tell me while I was in the States because they didn't think it was right after I'd just got married. Maybe they thought Jim was just going through a lean patch financially and they didn't want to make things any worse for him. Goodness gracious, he had us all fooled.

Things had changed since I'd been away. The Beatles had put Elvis's nose out of joint, but he was still 'The King' in my eyes. And The Rolling Stones were everywhere – I absolutely loved them.

Strange things were happening; times were changing. England won a World Cup and people were cock-a-hoop. Things were good, people were happy, and everybody seemed to have a job and plenty of time on their hands.

I got the vibe, but I couldn't partake. I dragged the past into the present like a tonne weight and couldn't let go. All my friends were married, settled down, but I felt like an outsider. I think some of them saw me as the Scarlet Woman; thought I might upset the apple cart and go after their husbands, which of course was absurd.

I was shunned, if truth be told. Not by all, but by many who didn't seem to want me around them even though they knew what had happened to me and that none of it was my fault. Maybe I got the wrong end of the stick, but I was definitely picking up vibes. I think they were truly sorry for what had happened, but I'd somehow lost that trust, just because I'd shacked up with some charlatan who I thought would give me a lifetime of happiness. At the same time, I felt a vague sense of loss for the baby that I knew I didn't want.

I was totally lost for things to do and people to see. One day I spotted an advert in The Gazette, the local paper. An amateur dramatics group were looking for actors for their theatre company, The Border Players of Yarm. I thought I might just have a go at that 'cos I'd always fancied myself as an actress and I was very good at drama at school. I'm so glad I did because I absolutely loved it and did two comedy plays with them. One was Cat Among the Pigeons where I played a French stripper. The play got rave reviews in the paper and in the cuttings it said that "Valerie Jackson couldn't have been any funnier if she'd tried".

I got even higher praise for the next play - the Sam Bate comedy End of the Honeymoon - as well as a standing ovation. I played this very posh woman called Vi Redfern who was part of a love triangle between the main character, his wife and two lovers. Vi, one of the "fiancees", was tee-total but she gets drunk on whisky after getting some shock news about her lover and I had to act out her drunken ramblings as she goes to confront the lousy swine who is already married. Naturally, I was well-versed in such a scenario and was made for the part.

The Gazette's theatre critic said the "exceptionally-polished" production was "rich in comedy" and that my handling of a "tipsy, uninhibited girl was skilful and hilarious".

To say we operated out of a small hut in Yarm (basically a social centre), we were very professional, and I really enjoyed my time with the Players. The only problem was they were real luvvie types. They hugged a lot and said things like, "Oh super, darling", which I didn't like. Me and Bill went out for a meal with them once and it was his worst nightmare.

"Don't ask me again," he said afterwards.

I hooked up with old friends from the Britannia Works who hadn't deserted me, and Bill was one of them. A crowd of us would go out on a Saturday night into town, to places like The Lord Raglan pub and have a good time and a few drinks. Some nights we'd head out to Saltburn on the coast to go for a dance at The Spa.

My old grammar-school friend Sue and her husband welcomed me into their home and couldn't have been nicer. Sue was one of the few people who never turned her back on me when I got back from the States. She understood.

With Bill and I, it was like we'd never been apart. His mother even let me sleep over, but in separate bedrooms. There was never yet a hint of romance: I'd got a new boyfriend and it didn't seem to bother Bill one bit.

One night, we all went to a party and I turned up with my boyfriend in his new sports car. We all got drunk and late into the night I went into the other room to get some food. Just as I was coming back through the door, Bill walked into the room and grabbed hold of me.

"What are you doing?" I said.

"I love you," he replied.

"Go away. I've been hurt enough."

But then we went into a big clinch and that was it.

"What are we going to do?" he said.

"Get married, I suppose," I said matter-of-factly.

It wasn't particularly romantic. I had to walk back into the party and say to my boyfriend that I was sorry but I just got engaged to Bill, and I intended to go home with him. He was speechless, but I'd rather be honest than deceitful. I'd turned up in his flashy sports car and ended up leaving in Bill's Morris Minor, but the old banger had character, just like my husband-to-be

.

The adoption couldn't officially go through until I got an annulment, which would render the marriage to Jim legally null and void, as if it never existed and was never valid in the first place. It was clearly an illegal marriage because, according to his mum, Jim already had several wives.

I got myself a lawyer and thought the annulment would be a piece of cake given Jim's prolific whoring, but the courts and the authorities put up a brick wall. They wouldn't accept it because of a lack of evidence against Jim. The very fact that it was transatlantic made the investigation painfully long and laborious, because the authorities had to piece together Jim's movements and trace his various concubines before he met me.

Three times the annulment was thrown out of court, each time because of a lack of evidence and the fact that Jim's serial womanising had occurred overseas. Luckily for me, his mother had given me the names of all the women he'd married and the towns where they had lived. I passed the details on to my solicitor who, after a long and exhaustive search, managed to track these women down and get them to sign an affidavit confirming they'd been married to Jim on the day he married me. Yet on his passport it said he was single, no children.

His photograph was sent out to all the sea ports and airports in the country, so that if he ever landed in the UK again he would be arrested for bigamy. The ball was finally rolling, but I just had this gut feeling that Jim would never get caught and that he would carry on whoring and notching up brides to his heart's content.

I had clearly misjudged him and it was plain that the only thing that could stop Jim was if he killed someone or somebody killed him. The bastard must have ruined countless lives and here was this little girl, the daughter he would never know or even care about, who had the promise of a good life but couldn't be granted official adoption status because there was no father's signature for it to go through.

Each time the annulment got thrown out of court in Teesside, so too did the adoption in the jurisdiction where the adoptive parents lived. I agonised over the future of the child and the anguish I was sure her adoptive parents were going through. I knew that they knew that I could change my mind at any moment and say I wanted my baby back. And I knew full well that until the annulment went through, they'd be fretting every time they got a letter through the post or a knock at the door. I just wanted to ring them and tell them I wasn't going to change my mind to give them reassurance, but I couldn't because the law wouldn't allow it, and you were not allowed to know their names or addresses.

I was determined the parents wouldn't have to go through any more agony, but the legal process dragged on. We went back to court, but the annulment got thrown out again. I burst into tears and the judge told me not to be too stressed! He said it would go ahead eventually and that they just needed more evidence from the United States.

I drew a line when I left Jim, but it began to dawn on me that this line was just a mirage. I was convinced he would haunt me forever; that I'd never really be rid of him. In fact, I was beginning to feel like I was the criminal.

I got legal aid as the annulment petitioner, but letters to me were headed 'Known as Mrs V. Bumbard', as if they were trying to rub salt into the wound. My solicitor had never seen anything like it. He was bewildered, which didn't fill me with a great deal of confidence. I don't think he knew what to do, to be honest.

Finally, they found some of Jim's previous wives which gave us the evidence we needed, and the annulment was granted. It had taken over a year to get the decree nisi, but it felt like another weight had been lifted off my shoulders. It also meant that my daughter's parents now knew that she was theirs by right, which was elation for me and I'm sure a massive relief for them.

The Adoption Society told me I could have pictures of the child sent to me as she grew up, but I said I didn't want them. Why would I want photographs when I'm trying to forget her? She was part of Jim, all wrapped up in the same parcel, and that part of my life was dead and buried as far as I was concerned.

It turned out that Jim had married again after I left the States. It had taken him less than two years to get hitched to some poor soul (I think it was his seventh wife) who was no doubt getting her poor head bashed in and realising, all too late, just what a terrible mistake she had made.

Bill and I decided to get married, but we had to wait six months for the decree absolute to come through. I told him from the outset that I didn't want any children. I said I'd had had such a bad time with the first child that I didn't want any more.

Bill seemed happy enough with this, but then, despite what I'd told the Adoption Society, I get photos of my daughter sent out to me and I start getting all broody again. There was one photo where she was walking, and they said she was a proper comedian, always singing and dancing, just like I did when I was a little girl.

I knew that if I'd have kept her, Bill would have treated her as one of his own because that's the kind of guy he is. Genuinely nice - the antithesis of Jim. And I was sure he would make a good husband.

I didn't want to get married in Middlesbrough because I'd married Jim at the registry office in town and I didn't want my day spoiled by horrible memories. Guisborough, 12 miles to the east, was the nearest registry office after Middlesbrough but I wanted to get married in church. They wouldn't let us because I'd been married before, even though I had done no wrong and they had no idea that my ex-husband was a polygamist, a wife-beater and a whore.

But the establishment wouldn't have it and we had to make do with a civil ceremony. Even that wasn't easy because I didn't live in the catchment area, but they finally relented when I gave them the address of an aunt who lived locally.

I was living at my nana's at the time 'cos my parents had moved to a new bungalow in the Yorkshire Dales. Nana helped me get ready on the morning of the wedding and I must say I did look rather nice.

My parents drove out to Middlesbrough to see me before I got wed. I was walking down the stairs when nana went to greet them as they opened the front door.

My father - who had put ribbons on the car and made it fit for a queen - took one look at me and said: "Oh, you look lovely, pet."

Mother, face like a wet mop, looked very much like she'd rather be somewhere else.

"You're lucky I'm here today," she sniffed. "I'm full of cold."

Mother had the air and manner of someone going to a funeral.

April 3, 1968 – which was just months apart from Jim's (alleged) sixth marriage and three days before my birthday - was a bitterly cold day and everyone was shivering as we had photos taken in the grounds of Guisborough Priory. There weren't many of us: just mother, father, my good friend Sue, who was maid of honour, Bill's parents and his best man, Eric, who had known Bill since he was five and went to the same school, Linthorpe Infants.

As the photographer lined us up for the photos, we were all shaking from the cold and Bill's knuckles went white. He was dying for a pee and told the cameraman to please hurry up. I look back at those old photos, see my mother and father in their finest, and I almost want to tear them up.

Mother didn't like Bill and he didn't like her. The two of them were uneasy in each other's company.

"He's too deep, him," she said. "You'll never know him."

She said he wouldn't make the right sort of husband, which was funny coming from a woman who wouldn't know what love was if it hit her straight between the eyes. This is the same woman, after all, who thought Jim was the bee's knees.

At first blush, it seemed that Bill was by no means perfect marriage material, and we weren't exactly what you'd call kindred spirits. He loved football and I hated the game. In fact, I hated all sports.

He was a bit staid, placid and introverted, whereas I was fiery, a bit extrovert and confrontational. He was mad about Middlesbrough Football Club whereas I didn't give a damn about my home team. But we gelled, we were a match. Opposites attract, they say, and we proved the point.

What I wanted more than anything, what I ached for, was security and trust, and I knew that Bill could provide those things in spades. I knew he'd never hit me and I knew he wouldn't be going out getting drunk every night. He'd been in the army and drunk with the best of them in his younger days, but I knew he was a good man with a good heart. A safe pair of hands.

We honeymooned in London, where Bill walked the legs off me. I hadn't been to London since the Festival of Britain in 1951, when I was six and totally in awe of the place.

Bill was one of those who stuck rigidly to his itinerary and his places to see. He was a proper tourist in that respect and we had to stick to the schedule. By the time we got to the National Portrait Gallery, I was knackered and had to sit down on a bench. The next thing I know I'm waking up with my head on a tramp's shoulder. And a disapproving museum official is looking down on me saying: "Excuse me, you can't sleep here."

He thought I was a bloody tramp. Apparently, this vagrant had sat down next to me while I was asleep. The museum guy must have thought I was the tramp's friend.

All I remember about London, apart from the embarrassing incident at the gallery, is tramping mile upon mile around the capital, looking for somewhere to rest. Bill had his schedule; I had feet which felt like they were sprouting bunions.

Bill was a true gentleman with a heart of gold, but good men with good hearts don't always have the best of luck and within three weeks of the marriage, he would find this out.

Chapter 10

Keep an Eye out for the Road Ahead

Our first house was a poky mid-terrace in town which was so cold in the winter there was ice on the inside of the windows. You got dressed very quickly.

We moved in as soon as we got married but we had to fit an inside toilet before we could get a mortgage. There was just a bath and a sink in the bathroom, which took up half of one of the two bedrooms – a sort of accidental en suite, if you like.

There was a decent lounge at the front and an open coal fire, but it was basic to the core and we spent all our time in the back room and kitchen. The only toilet was out in the yard and Middlesbrough in winter is not the sort of place where you want to be visiting an outside loo, so we got these plumbers in to install an indoor toilet and the building society agreed to the loan.

The previous owner was an elderly lady who had turned the back yard into a lovely little ornate garden which had arches and plants and things. I thought it was wonderful.

Bill was earning £16 a week as a store clerk at the Cleveland Works and I was working for my father's business, earning £8 a week. A joint income of £24 a week was barely enough to run a house, but strangely enough, we never seemed to want for anything.

If truth be told, we didn't have two pennies to rub together and Bill had to sell his Morris 1100 so we could buy some second-hand furniture. He didn't get much for it, but it allowed us to scratch enough together to furnish the house to an extent.

Mother and father had moved to a quaint little dales village called Scruton, between Bedale and Northallerton, where they'd bought a nice, two-bedroom bungalow. They invited us for Sunday lunch a few weeks after we got married and we drove there with our family friend, Bob Lewis, in his car.

When we arrived in Scruton I was immediately smitten by the place. It was a gorgeous little country village which had an old pub, an 11th-century church and an air of quiet gentility. I imagined my parents felt like this was where they belonged in the general hierarchy of things. They had this massive lounge and nice gardens. It was indeed an impressive residence.

Opposite the bungalow on the main road was a field that was empty apart from what looked like an old church or school room. There are houses there now. They always spoil things, don't they?

Mother cooked a sumptuous Sunday lunch, as was her wont, and the afternoon passed quite agreeably. Bill was never comfortable in her presence, but she was a picture of politeness that day. The snide comments were always made behind his back.

The intention was to drive on to a farm in Bedale four miles away, to visit a family friend who had given us a nice wedding present which I think was bedding of some kind. Bill and I always made sure we returned favours and we wanted to thank her in person.

Father lent me his brand-new Vauxhall Viva SL90, which he'd only had two weeks. We set off for Bedale and had just reached Leeming Bar, just a few miles from the farm, when it happened.

We were coming out of a 30mph zone on the Bedale road, into a 'No Speed Limit' section underneath the A1, when I turned to Bill and said: "I'll put me foot down; let's see how this car goes."

Before I got the chance to step on the gas, I saw this other car driving towards us in the opposite direction. Without stopping, the driver tried to turn off to the right and came straight towards us. Surely, he must stop. We had right of way. But he didn't look like he was going to stop. He was coming right at us.

"God forgive me everything I've done; I'm on my way," I said.

Bill jumped forward in his seat and screamed: "The bastard isn't going to stop! The bas..."

When it hit, it was like a juggernaut had smashed into us, head-on. The guy's young daughter flew out the windscreen and Bill head-butted the dashboard. The impact was so fierce both cars were lifted into the air and ended up on the wrong side of the road.

The dashboard went straight through Bill's mouth. There were no seat belts back then, which meant there was nothing to prevent or cushion the blow. The windscreen was smashed to smithereens and Bill's mouth basically chomped the dashboard and it split his face wide open at a cross angle. He was screaming out: a horrible, high-pitched shriek that made my blood freeze. Blood was just oozing from him. I was in shock; dazed and trapped because I couldn't open my door. But I felt in one piece.

Bill grabbed hold of me and dragged me out his side because the driver's door had caved in. We clambered out, but then Bill almost collapsed. He was hanging over the car, holding onto the roof because he couldn't stand. Blood continued to pour from the huge gash which had split his head and mouth open. He had a huge cut to his right eye which was horrifically swollen, and his top lip had been torn apart.

I felt blood trickle down my face, but I was more concerned for Bill. I knew I wasn't seriously injured: the steering wheel, which was at right angles, had saved me.

Someone ran into a cottage nearby to call an ambulance. I was in a state of utter panic and Bill was crying out. I dashed into the cottage and asked the owner if I could ring my parents. He said, "of course", but when I rang the number there was no reply. I assumed they must have been out walking the dog or something. I left the man their number and asked him to keep ringing until they answered.

"Will you ring them and tell them we'll be at the Friarage Hospital in Northallerton?"' I pleaded.

He nodded and looked at me, with much sympathy but mostly bewilderment. I was crazed, frantic.

I must have been hysterical running out of the cottage 'cos a woman slapped me across the face, telling me to get a hold of myself, and asked me if I wanted a cigarette. I took the cigarette off her which brought me to my senses momentarily, but I was sobbing uncontrollably.

I took quick, frantic puffs on the tobacco, then dashed back to the mangled wreckage where my husband's broken face was painted a claret red. We waited for the ambulance.

The paramedics were calm and reassuring. They put Bill on a stretcher and I got in the back of the ambulance with him. The ambulance staff told me not to panic but I cried all the way to the hospital. They passed me a foot pump and told me to keep pressing on it to drain the blood from Bill's mouth, so he didn't swallow any. I was pumping that thing like mad all the way to the hospital, with every last drop of energy I had left, terrified that Bill would choke on his own blood if I relaxed for a second.

The ambulance pulled into the hospital and Bill was stretchered out. He wasn't moving and blood was oozing from his face. People were saying stupid things like, "Oh, he must have a hole in his chest", which pushed me over the edge.

I turned to the paramedics and pleaded with them: "Please fix him, we've only been married three weeks".

They took him straight to emergency and I was in bits in the waiting room. I bawled me eyes out and people stared.

I had three stitches inserted in my eyebrow and I was bruised across my chest, but the injuries were all psychological with me. The other driver's daughter was taken to the Friarage but not seriously hurt, despite going through the windscreen.

The owner of the cottage had been as good as his word and phoned my father, who drove over from Scruton as soon as he heard.

The police told my father to go and collect his belongings from the car before they got towed away. Father told me he'd paddled through pools of blood to get to the car and was certain that at least one of us was dead.

I waited for him at the hospital with more desperation than I'd waited for him in the States - and that was pretty desperate.

Father's SL90, his two-week-old pride and joy, was a crumpled wreck and obviously a right-off, but I don't remember him saying anything about it when he arrived at the hospital and found me in floods of tears outside the operating theatre. Once again, he had come to my rescue when I needed him most.

We waited interminable hours, praying that someone would come out of theatre with a smile and good news. Finally, a doctor walked up to us. He looked slightly grave but said that Bill had come though okay. They'd put 60 stitches inside and outside his mouth but were hopeful they could save the eye by stitching it.

His eye had been caught by smashed glass. We didn't know whether it was from his glasses or the windscreen, but some glass had got into his eye and the cut was very bad. We found his glasses with no lenses at the crash scene.

We were quite relieved by the prognosis but very scared and uncertain. Father drove me back to Scruton and I spent the night there in quiet, tearful despair. I don't think I slept a wink and even my mother was strangely quiet. She appeared deeply concerned. Apparently, she waited until I'd gone to bed, then hand-washed the blood off Bill's clothes.

The following day I crawled out of bed with a head like lead and dreaded what they were going to tell us at the hospital. I hardly touched my breakfast and then father got out the mini-van which he used for work. He ushered me out onto the driveway.

"You're driving to the hospital," he said.

"No, I'm not," I replied.

"Yes, you are."

"No, I'm not."

"You are."

"I don't want to drive," I pleaded.

"Get in there, ya bastard," he said. And practically shoved me in.

It took my breath away, but it was the best thing he ever did because if he hadn't made me get back behind the wheel, I don't think I would ever have driven again. He shouted at me on purpose 'cos he knew if I didn't drive that day, I'd be catching buses or hailing taxis for the rest of my life.

I drove, but it was a torrid experienced. My hands were glued to the steering wheel, my knuckles were white, the whole way up the A19. And all the while my parents' Labrador, Kirkdale - named after a picturesque valley near Bedale, in keeping with my parents' delusions of grandeur - was licking my neck in the back seat.

Every time a car pulled out from the left I froze and my heart rate shot through the roof because I was terrified they wouldn't stop. I'd veer out into the middle of the road and turn the car around in a semi-circle. I was petrified, a nervous wreck, and I'd not even changed clothes. My skirt was covered in blood 'cos I'd not brought any spares. We were only supposed to visit my parents and their friend for the day. How could we ever have envisioned such a horrifying outcome?

Bill was lying still and lifeless when we got there. His face was crushed, terribly scarred, and I felt like he would never be able to look at me the same way again - if at all.

He couldn't see out of his right eye, but he was conscious throughout, and strangely, felt no pain. The doctors told him it was the shock and adrenaline that dulled the pain, but still the blood spewed out of him. He lost six pints and we were getting frantic again.

He was kept in The Friarage for a few days and then transferred to Hunden's Lane Hospital in Darlington, where there was a specialist eye surgeon. They pumped six pints of blood into him to replenish the stock and stitched his eye, but it looked like he would lose it.

The specialist came to the bed and with his minions and he was talking about removing the eye, but then one of the nurses switched the light on and Bill said: "Did you switch a light on there 'cos I could see that?".

He was supposed to have the eye out the following day, but after he noticed the light, the surgeon changed his mind and the operation was cancelled. They left it a couple of days and then sent us home.

We couldn't kiss for months because the nerve ends around Bill's mouth were dead. The medical term they gave us was "unable to osculate". How romantic.

I was now Bill's carer as well as his new wife. I had to shave him, which was when I discovered they'd forgotten to remove one of his stitches. I sterilised a pair of scissors and took it out.

We got him an out-patients' appointment at Middlesbrough Infirmary and they did eye-prism tests. When they shone the light on him, Bill pointed in the opposite direction and said the light was coming from "here", but it was shining the other way. He was clearly impaired, so the doctors said they'd have to take the eye out.

They told us that if they didn't remove the bad eye, Bill could go blind in both because the muscles at the back were connected. They told us they'd have to keep him in overnight and sent me home to get his toiletries. The operation was set for the following day.

We were devastated and I cried again, but Bill remained philosophical and seemingly unperturbed. The next day they took his eye out and I went to visit him with some trepidation. And there he was, laid in bed, very calm.

When visiting was over, he said to me: "OK, you can go now."

"Bill, none of the visitors are leaving; it's alright," I said.

"The sister said I could watch the football," he replied.

He was dying to watch the European Cup Final between Manchester United and Benfica and seemed more interested in that than me. I smiled and thought: "He's ok."

I shook my head and said: "There's nothing wrong with you. I'm going home."

When Bill came home they gave us this plastic thing to put in his socket to keep it in shape until he got his new eye. They gave me a special tool to take the plastic 'eye' out. I did this every day, then I had to wash it and pop it back in again. Not a particularly pleasant thing to do, but I just did it.

Bill was off work for months and had to get sick notes off his doctor whom he'd known for years. After a while, he got bored with not being at work and said to the doctor: "I'm alright now."

But the doctor says: "You're not going back to work until you get fitted with an artificial eye."

Bill was quite ill at one point because of all the medication he was taking. They'd given him hundreds of tablets, mainly sedatives, but it was far too big a dose. The sedation was so strong he kept falling asleep and he was bumping into people all the time because he couldn't see out of his right side.

"Watch where you're going mate!" they'd say. And not in a nice way.

I was consumed by guilt because it was me who had been driving the car. As with my marriage to Jim, I knew deep down that it wasn't my fault, but you always blame yourself. All kinds of things were going through my head, silly thoughts like if Bill hadn't married me, he wouldn't have been in the car and he wouldn't have lost his eye.

Such was my guilt complex that for months after the crash I kept asking him: "Are you sure you love me?"

"Of course I love you," he'd say.

And I'd reply: "Well, if you hadn't married me, you'd have two eyes now."

Bill had an appointment with this woman at Crown House in Middlesbrough where he had to pick out a new eye and get it fitted. She had what looked like a tool box, divided into sections, inside which were hundreds of plastic eyes of every colour. Very creepy, like they were looking at you. It was, to all intents and purposes, an 'eye shop'. A very macabre sort of browsing experience.

The woman was picking eyes out of the box and holding them up, musing over them while looking over at Bill and trying to find a match.

"Look at the colour and the size of them," she told him.

She was a perfectionist, a dealer in fake eyes, and may I say she was a true professional, a master of her chosen field.

At length she found one she thought was a perfect match and popped it straight in. All done and dusted: Bill's got two eyes again.

I was working at my father's office the day he got his eye fitted. After leaving the 'eye shop', he came straight to the office and I gasped: "You've got two eyes!"

It looked so strange after all that time wearing the plastic support. An unnerving experience: I just couldn't get used to Bill with two eyes.

The driver who'd bashed into us was charged with driving without due care and attention, and the case went to court in Bedale. We all had to give evidence in the witness box because the guy had pleaded not guilty. He's got all that evidence stacked against him and yet he's making us relive the whole thing again.

It turned out that the guy, who was a teacher, had been talking to his young daughter in the moments before the crash. She'd been feeling sick and he was looking at her instead of the road when we crashed head-on.

We couldn't believe what we were hearing. Just seconds before the crash, the guy had turned round to his daughter and said: "Well, we're going to Leeming Hotel and I'll get you a drink."

They put me on the stand and the guy's barrister tried to make out I was too young and inexperienced to drive. He even claimed I was on the wrong side of the road when the car hit us because that's where both vehicles ended up. Luckily for us, we had a witness who testified on our behalf. He was from Billingham, not far from Middlesbrough.

He'd stopped at the scene and I gave him my name and address. He told the court that no way were we on the wrong side of the road; that the impact was so big that both vehicles were catapulted onto the other side. His testimony destroyed the defence case and the guy ended up changing his plea to guilty.

He was clearly bang to rights and then the court hears about Bill's dreadful injuries. It could so easily have been fatal, but the judge gives the guy a £10 fine and I don't think he even got a driving ban. This was 1968 and things were different. Nowadays, he'd have been banned for at least three years and got a heavy fine for causing serious injury through careless driving. Maybe even a suspended prison sentence.

The Gods must have been smiling down on him from the moment he was born. He came out of the crash with barely a scratch and his daughter was pretty much unscathed despite going through the windscreen. Of course, we were relieved the little girl was okay, but I did feel like her father had got away with murder.

As we were leaving court, we came across him and he looked contrite. He looked over at us and said: "I really couldn't remember what happened, and then I realised it was my fault after I heard the evidence."

I was looking at him thinking that I wanted to knife him, but then Bill says to him: "How's your daughter?"

That's Bill for you – soft as putty. The guy could have killed us, Bill's lost an eye, and he asks him how his daughter is!

Chapter 11

Too Posh to Push

I was still grappling with the after-effects of my nightmare in the States when my new husband became my one-eyed husband just three weeks into the marriage. My daughter's gone, Bill can't work, and Jim still lurks in the shadows. Did he still think about me? I doubted it and sincerely hoped not.

I look back now and think: how did I get through it all? But you just do. And the reason is because you have no other option.

No other choice because Jim can't be allowed to win, Bill needs help and I'm pregnant again. I'd got very broody after the adoption and I knew for certain I wanted another child.

About two months into the pregnancy, we moved to a nice new house in Acklam, a few miles out of town. It was a big, three-bedroomed semi in Trimdon Avenue with separate bathroom and toilet, a large dining room and a big garden. It cost us £4,200, but I knocked them down £200 because it had an asbestos garage and it would have cost us £200 to have a brick one built. Peanuts, really. How times have changed.

Bill returned to work before Victoria was born and with my secretarial work at father's place, we were pulling in a decent income. Finally, the money for the car crash came through as well. We got £5,000, which doesn't sound a lot now, but it was quite a lot of money back then and we used it to buy the house. I think we claimed off the other guy's insurance, which was a victory of sorts since he'd got off virtually scot-free.

I went to the solicitors to get the cheque and was supposed to meet Bill there, but the dozy sod forgot.

I rang him at work and said: "Where are you Bill?"

"At work. Why?"

"'Cos I'm at the bloody solicitors waiting for this cheque!"

It was like winning the pools for us and Bill couldn't even remember to go and sign for it!

We put £2,500 down as deposit on the house, bought a brand-new car - a Mini - and furnished and carpeted our new home. And when it was all done, we took all our friends and family out for a meal.

It was a relief to get out of the freezing, two-up, two-down terrace in town, which we never really got used to and quite frankly couldn't stand. Eighteen months in that place was 18 months too long, and it was no place to bring up a baby.

I dreaded giving birth after the horrible experience I'd had with Hazel at Parkside, so this time we went private. We chose a hospital in Stockton which had the best facilities, the best maternity staff and the best doctors. The consultant I chose, Mr Shepherd, was based there.

I was two weeks overdue and had to be induced. When I got the first pains I gripped the rails and yelled: "What the bloody hell am I doing here? I know what it's like! I've been through it before! I must be bloody mad!"

The nurse came in and said: "Mrs Yare, you're waking everybody up!"

They wouldn't let me push at first because I was a private patient. We had to wait for Mr Shepherd to come in. They kept putting this gas and air on me, but I kept pushing it away. It was quite comical really.

"You can't push yet – you're a private patient!" they said.

Yes, I bloody am! It wasn't a Caesarean and the baby was ready to come out.

Mr Shepherd got the forceps out and she slid out like a bar of soap. It was painless; so easy.

I heard this baby cry and said: "Somebody's had a baby in here!"

The nurses laughed and one of them said: "Ooh, 'ark at her!"

Mr Shepherd said proudly: "This lady had a terrible time with her first birth and she can't believe it was so uncomplicated this time."

It was June 6, 1970 - the 25th anniversary of D-Day. We called it Delivery Day.

We named her Victoria Louise. She was a fortnight late and, to be honest, she's been late ever since. I couldn't believe she'd been born: it was so quick and she was Bill's double - all 7lb 1oz of her.

Mother came in to see me and she too noted the striking similarities between Bill and Victoria.

"Don't worry," she said, "you can always get her cosmetic surgery."

That was the thing about mother - always so tactful.

Nobody had been allowed in before the birth. It wasn't the done thing back then and I wouldn't have wanted them in there anywhere. I think it's the most degrading position for a woman to be in.

Little Victoria was my new world. We wrapped her in cotton wool and her only danger was her father's hazy vision. He couldn't see at all on his right side and kept tripping over her as she crawled around on the floor. I lost count of the number of times he nearly stood on her, but mercifully he never did. When we were round at my nana's she'd make him a cup of tea and pass it over his right shoulder, right in the blind spot. The tea would go flying and there was not a damn thing any of us could do about it. Nana just couldn't get it right, bless her, and Bill couldn't bloody see her.

Victoria was only five weeks old when she became desperately ill. She was screaming and throwing up her breast milk and I was utterly terrified because I didn't know what the hell was wrong with her. We called a doctor out but were still no wiser, so we took her to hospital and when they took her nappy off she was red raw. They more or less accused me of neglect and I, of course, went ballistic at such a ridiculous accusation.

It turned out she had a urine infection and they kept her in hospital for a week. It was a nightmare for me because I had to get up early and breastfeed her at the hospital, then go to work, then go back at dinnertime to breastfeed her again, then go back to work again. By the time I arrived back home to give Bill his tea, I was out on my feet – and I still had to go back and feed her before bed.

Victoria was Christened at St Mary's Church in Acklam two days after she got out of Middlesbrough General Hospital. She was back to full health and sleeping beautifully. You could put your clock by her in the afternoon: out like a light at 1.30pm, wide awake by 3 o'clock. A brass band could have been playing and she'd have slept through it. I even Hoovered around her and she never stirred.

We watched her grow into a curious and intelligent child and my mind flashed back to her half-sister - my present from Jim who was now a mystery to me. I tried to put her out of my mind, but that shock of ruby-red hair and thumbs just like mine were images too vivid to cast aside.

Victoria went to Kader Infants School just up the road and showed all the signs of being a very bright and vivacious child. We got her a live-in nanny because we both worked. I had my hands full at father's place and Bill was still getting used to working with a plastic eye. He got promoted to stores manager at the Cargo Fleet Works near South Bank, where he was put in charge of stock-taking and ordering.

Just before Victoria was born, I got promoted to company secretary and director of father's business. As a director, I had to shoulder a great deal of responsibility, whereas before I just looked after the accounts in the office. I didn't know it then, but there were people at the company who were far from happy with my promotion, and my mother, who was also a director, was one of them. I knew something was afoot, but I didn't know quite what.

I noticed mother eyeing me with deep suspicion. Did she really think I was trying to take the place over? Quite possibly yes, in her mind.

Maybe I was paranoid, overwrought with the weight of the past. But I just had this feeling something sinister was underway.

The truth is that I was just an extremely hard worker and took great pride in my work, but I was never ambitious or avaricious. I was a perfectionist, I was punctilious, and everything had to be just so, but I never had designs above my station and I was never a usurper.

I knew it then and I'll say it now: I was effectively running the show because father was always away, 'meeting' people. And, generally, people don't like to see others excel and get on. It breeds jealousy and mistrust.

Mother was clearly no fan of mine, but in her eyes, Bill was an even lower specimen. Her appraisal was confirmed (at least in her mind) when Bill got blotto at my parents' Silver Wedding anniversary. We'd been out for a meal at the Golden Lion in Northallerton, but when we returned to their house for drinks, my parents stupidly put Bill in charge of the bar and he got stuck into the liqueur like he was back in the army. He got horribly drunk and by the end of the night he slid down a wall and his false eye popped out. The look of disgust on mother's face was priceless.

Because he'd lost his bottom eyelid in the accident, he had to keep wiping his eye 'cos there was nowhere for the tears to go. If he didn't keep wiping it, the eye would fill up with tears and there was always a danger it could fall out. Well, he was that bloody drunk he kept forgetting to wipe his eye. It slid out and fell on the floor, bouncing across the carpet. I was looking under the chair for it and, thank God, I found the thing staring up at me. I picked it up, spat on it and rubbed it on my dress. I shot Bill a look and said: "Get that bloody thing put back in - now!"

He slid it back in the socket as people covered their mouths in horror. Mother shook her head; dad frowned. Bill - two-eyed again - smiled drunkenly, utterly oblivious to the shock and awe all around him.

If I thought Bill couldn't have got any lower in mother's estimations, he proved us all wrong that night, but of course he was such a good man and I knew he was right for me. Eye-popping calamities aside, we were very comfortable with each other, we were financially stable and we had a lovely daughter to dote on. Plus, Bill was about to become a 70's fashion icon, with hair down to his shoulders and a thick, luxurious tash like Tom Selleck. He wore flowery shirts, flairs and platform shoes. Yowzer!

Mother came to the house one day with the look of a shell-shock victim, all pale and gnarled. Something was horribly wrong and I guessed from the furrowed brow and the pained expression that it had something to do with my father.

"Do you know he's been having an affair?" she said. "He's had other women."

"Yes, I know."

"Well, why didn't you tell me?"

"Because I didn't want to upset you."

I don't know who told her about the affairs, or whether she found out by herself. After all, it was plain bleeding obvious he'd been playing around. But when she found out, she went berserk and father called the police out. She came straight round to confront me. She said he was crazy for calling the police.

"He's mad; he needs certifying," she said.

She asked me to sign a form to have him certified, but I refused.

"You sign it," I said. "He's your bloody husband."

For once, cracks were beginning to show on that otherwise stiff, unmoved face. She looked at me much as a puppy might look at his owner when he wants feeding. She seemed to want some kind of answer from me, but what answer could I possibly give her? Anyone could have told her that her husband was a cad and a rotter.

Yet part of me thought there's no wonder father strayed with a wife like that, although it was still unforgiveable. She was, after all, a frightful old bitch and I didn't feel sorry for her one bit. It wasn't getting even; it wasn't even just desserts. I was simply unmoved because of the woman she was.

I may have felt no sympathy for mother, but it crushed me personally 'cos I looked on my father as a deity. What she couldn't get over, what really gnawed away at her, was that I'd known about his infidelities for some time and didn't tell her. What was the point? It would only upset her, and besides, she liked the lifestyle.

Oh mother, how little you knew. And the reason I knew that she knew so little was because my father had come onto me. Just the once, but strange and skin-crawling nonetheless.

It happened a few years prior to my mother finding out about father's affairs, but I only reveal it now because to have done so earlier would have been to besmirch a man I looked up to as a saint and who, at the time, could do no wrong in my eyes.

We were driving back from somewhere when he pulled into a layby and put his arms around me.

"What are you doing?" I said.

I pushed him off and, unbelievably, he looked surprised.

"Get off!" I said, pushing him away. "I'm your daughter!"

And that was that. Without so much as a word, he put the car into gear and drove off. And then he starts chatting to me as if nothing had happened, jabbering away all the way home about this and that! It didn't bother him one bit that he'd just made a pass at his own daughter. It was as if he'd just erased it from his memory the second it was over. He was God's gift after all, and I suppose in his mind I was just another potential conquest, one of a succession of ladies who should have bowed to his will and given him what he wanted.

When all's said and done, he was a weedy little man, quite ugly, but he had the money, the bravado and supreme self-confidence which had ordinarily-self-respecting women falling at his feet. He was ballsy, cocky and utterly selfish. Such traits can endear certain types of women to certain kinds of men.

It was a stinking rotten thing to do to your own daughter, but I just brushed it off for the sake of my sanity and buried my head in the sand.

Father clearly had the morals of a sewer rat, but surely even rodents don't stoop that low? Rats will do many revolting things, but as far as I know, they do not make a pass at their own children.

I remember thinking that I'd have to be more careful in future about where I went with my friends if father was in tow. I even worried about Victoria in case he tried it on with her when she got a bit older.

Father's libido knew no bounds and he didn't draw the line anywhere. He made a beeline for my friends and I have no doubt he would have bedded any one of them given the chance.

One day, when we were all in the pub, he made a pass at my best friend. He must have done it so discreetly because I had no idea at the time, but she told me afterwards. We'd been friends since school and she told me everything.

"Oh no," I said. "That's awful."

"Yeah," she said. "If I'd have told my husband, he'd have killed him."

My mother was in the pub at the time, but nothing would stand in the way of my father and potential concubines. It was fair game, and he was insatiable.

I didn't want to believe it, even *refused* to believe it. But then he made a pass at another one of my friends when we were all out for a drink. I looked away 'cos I couldn't bear to look.

He tried to kiss her. He was twice her age, for goodness' sake. It was cringeworthy. My mother wasn't there this time, but I saw it alright.

I'd suspected he was up to no good for a year or two, ever since I started taking his calls as company secretary. These weren't business calls: these were the unmistakable voices of my mother's friends – father's floozies. And that's when the penny dropped.

There were four or five affairs, but those were just the ones I knew about – and all were mother's friends. I'm sure there was a lot more, but it seems mother never picked up on the signs or at least chose to ignore them. He was a high-earning man after all, and she enjoyed a good life with him.

Maybe father wanted a slimmer figure. Mother was quite a large woman; her figure wasn't attractive. She ended up dyeing her hair blonde, but she was actually a brunette and the older she got, the bigger she became. This can spell trouble for a woman of a certain size and appearance when your husband's got money, if not looks.

When she was younger, she looked like Bette Davis, but that's no compliment because Davis was no looker either. What Davis had was charisma and incredible acting ability, neither of which was in mother's repertoire.

One day at the workplace, father finally gave up the pretence after so many years whoring around. Well, he knew he couldn't hide it from me anymore because I'd become his call-taker for all his mistresses. Once I knew about one, he just came clean and admitted the lot. Actually, he bragged about it. Yes, he was boasting. Can you believe that? A man boasting to his daughter that he'd messed around behind his wife's back. And it turned out that this wasn't just a few dizzy bimbos on the side: father was in it for the long haul. He'd been at it for years.

To think he'd managed to hide it from us all those years and no-one suspected a thing. And I'd thought father was the antidote to Jim - angel and devil, if you like. But in many ways, they were kindred spirits, highly-skilled operators in their own seedy little way. Whorers, charlatans, conmen both.

I put my father on a pedestal. Once the mask dropped and the myth was exposed, my life was shattered. As horrid as he was, Jim was just a bit-player in my life's turmoil compared with father. Jim's con may have been ruthless, totally illegal and utterly immoral, but father's deceptions would leave a much deeper mark than any of the beatings Jim dished out. Compared with my father's lifetime of deceit, Jim's cruel hoax was ephemeral and the scars would eventually heal. It was practically a sideshow.

It was almost as if, now I was an adult, father thought he may as well come clean and let me in on his secret. He obviously had not an ounce of shame, no compunction in telling me about his many flings and dalliances. We were very close, after all, and perhaps he thought I wouldn't mind. Maybe he thought that because I didn't get on with my mother, I wouldn't tell her. He was right, I didn't tell her, but only to spare her feelings.

Or maybe it's just because he was a cocky bastard who didn't care a fig whether I knew or not. Perhaps he felt invincible, what with all his money, the successful business and all these people at his beck and call, obeying his every command. And all these mistresses who'd satisfied him despite his dwarfish ugliness and plain-speaking manner, they must have liked his money because there was nothing else attractive about him. He was a little man with red, wavy hair and a moustache.

When he went up to Ohio on that business trip after he picked me up in Louisiana, he met some guys at a factory and they invited him round to their houses for meals with their families. One of them introduced my father to his children and one of the boys said: "He sure sounds like a Beatle, but he sure don't look like one!"

Father had one big thing going for him (no, not that - at least not as far as I know). His one big thing was that he always carried a wad-full of cash around with him - but it wasn't his money. Oh no, it was the business's money that he hadn't banked. But he always flashed it about as if it was his, no doubt to impress the ladies.

Money attracts a certain kind of woman and my father had plenty of it. I can think of no other reason why they would fall at his feet given he was just 5ft 6in and so ill-favoured in the looks department. Perhaps he *was* hung like a donkey - I'll never know. Daughters don't ask those kinds of questions of their fathers. That would be repulsive and abhorrent, in anyone's estimation.

Not long after my father made a pass at me on the layby, I started developing a phobia of cats. It was strange.

I had no idea why I should be so scared of these creatures, albeit I was never a big fan. I'm more of a dog person.

After all, when I first met Bill, his mam and dad had one which used to sit on my knee. But it got to the stage where I couldn't bear to be in the presence of one, not even in the same vicinity. It freaked me out.

Every time I had to go and see someone I would ring them first and ask if they had any cats in the house. Usually, mercifully, they'd say: "No, we have a dog."

And I would breathe a sigh of relief. I think they thought I was just allergic to cats, but the problem was far more serious than that. It was clinical: a pathological fear.

A real phobia is terrible because you have no control over it. I couldn't even bear to look at a cat in a magazine or a newspaper. I had it really bad, so I decided to go and see a psychologist and paid to go private. He was very confident he could cure me and said he'd once cured a guy of a giraffe phobia.

"Well, you see a lot of them around here, don't you?" I said.

Apparently, this guy with the giraffe phobia was a gamekeeper in Africa and once ran one over. It was neck and neck as to whose was the weirdest phobia.

I saw the psychologist once a week and he asked me all kinds of questions, but my irrational fear completely baffled him.

"I can't understand you," he said. "You've got a fur coat on, so it can't be the fur that is troubling you."

Back then, nobody thought twice about buying real fur 'cos everyone did it and we weren't as enlightened as we are today. I wouldn't dream of wearing a real fur coat now.

"How do you feel about stuffed cats?" he said.

"I think they should all be bloody stuffed," I replied.

"Oh," he says, "I was thinking about bringing a stuffed cat for the next time you come."

"You do that and you'll never survive," I said.

Then he tried semi-hypnotising me and played tapes of cats meowing, but nothing worked.

Weeks passed by and we were still no wiser. I just resigned myself to the fact that I'd have to avoid every cat in the world for the rest of my life, even if it meant running home with my shopping and knocking little kids over. But then we had a breakthrough 'cos I finally began to trust him and started to open up. There's no point going to see a shrink if you don't tell him everything. If you hold things back, you'll not get anywhere. Besides, you're paying the guy!

The psychologist said to me one night: "Which of the cats do you hate the most?"

"Ginger ones."

"And what colour's your father's hair?"

"Ginger."

Bingo!

Once we'd established the root cause, the shrink replayed the tapes of cats meowing and said to me: "If you see a cat, instead of getting worked up, say to yourself: 'Calm and serene... calm and serene.'"

The next day I walked into this shop and I heard a meow. I turned around and saw this bloody thing staring right at me with piercing green eyes. I turned around and ran at double speed out of the shop. Calm and serene went out the window.

I went back in to see my shrink and told him about my experience in the store in town. He told me that the phobia was persisting because my father was still alive. When he died, it would all be over.

"When your father dies, I'm not saying you'll be able to pick a cat up and stroke it, but I would say that you'll be able to tolerate them," he said.

And then he said something which really struck home, and he explained it really well.

"A phobia is something that's dormant in your mind," he said. "So, you see a cat and you walk around it. The next time you see one, you've got to cross the road. And then that's one up to your phobia and eventually you get to the stage where you cannot be anywhere near them – your phobia has won."

My first test came a few days later when I went out to the shops with Victoria. We'd just parked the car and were walking across the road when she suddenly tugged at my coat and said: "Look – there's a cat over there, mam."

I grabbed hold of her and dashed to the other side of the street in about 0.8 seconds. When we were safely on the pavement, a good distance away from the cat, Victoria started rubbing her arm which had scratch marks on it. I must have dug my nails into her when she cried "Cat!". If truth be told, I'd climb walls if I saw them in the street.

These psychologists know the score: they're very intelligent people and they've seen it all before. They'd dealt with much stranger phobias than mine and they never doubt your fears, but equally they tell you not to hide from them; you must confront the underlying issue. Believe it or not, there are people out there with a fear of grass (agrostophobia); a phobia about buttons (koumpounophobia); and people who are scared stiff of sand (ammophobia). There's a phobia for everything, I suppose.

"Who else do you see?" I asked my shrink.

"Oh, people who have problems with their marriage and that."

"Oh, sex life?" I asked.

"Yeah, that's it."

"What do you do? Read sexy books to them?"

But he was right all along about the ginger cats. He put it all into perspective for me, even though it didn't really help. Diagnosis doesn't cure irrational fear - it only explains it.

Any cat could scare me senseless, but it was the ginger ones that really put the fear of God in me.

The psychologist had got it spot on and it all made perfect sense: the deceitful father figure with ginger hair had repulsed me, and by extension, sly, ginger felines terrified me. Yet it seemed that this fear of mine was not only derivative - brought on by my father's abhorrent behaviour - but also genetic.

My mother said that when she was pregnant with me, and living at her mother's, a cat once jumped out at her from a privet hedge. She'd never liked cats and was frightened of them, so this really freaked her out.

I can look at them now in a book or see them on TV and it makes me upset if they're hurt, so I guess that's a bit of an improvement, but I don't think I'd like to be in the same room or even the same house as one. I've got a lot better since father died, but the phobia's still there. I would love to be able to get over it, but cats still terrify me.

In all honesty, they appal me. They're my worst nightmare - if you discount Jim and my father.

Chapter 12

Goodbye Val

Bill and I had gone round to my parents' for Sunday tea when I dropped the bombshell. We'd taken Victoria with us. I told my father he should retire from the company.

"Why don't you pack it in?" I said. "You're never there. Why don't you retire, take on a golden handshake?"

He put his knife and fork down, stirred in his chair and looked back at me. I was expecting him to hit the roof, but remarkably he seemed unfazed.

"Oh, that's something to think about," he said. "That's a good idea."

I was taken aback, but then I saw mother's murderous expression which was burning a hole through my forehead and I knew there'd be hell to pay.

When I got back to work I mentioned my proposal to the other directors and they suggested we send father a letter formally asking him to resign. The letter was sent out and father's immediate reaction was to go and see his solicitor to plot my downfall in the company. Not the other directors - just me, his daughter, the agitator.

His response - no doubt encouraged by his solicitor - was that he had no intention of stepping down and woe betide anyone who should try to persuade him otherwise. Yet he was never at work; he'd let go of the reins and left it to others to run the ship - mainly me. If an important decision had to be made, he was never there to make it. I watched him come and go; I noticed he'd be off 'on business' when there was nothing in the diary. Where was he going? And more to the point, who was he going to see?

On reflection, I think he didn't want to retire because he couldn't stand the thought of being at home with mother all day.

I'd pitched retirement to my father with a degree of trepidation knowing how obstinate and high-handed he could be, but I could never have imagined the speed and ruthlessness with which he tried to engineer my dismissal. I should have known better: such impertinence wasn't tolerated in father's world, nor mother's, for that matter. They called the shots and I was certain she had a hand in this.

The atmosphere in the office was toxic, but father kept his cards close to his chest. I thought maybe he'd forgotten about my proposal, but, oh, how wrong I was. He never forgets anything, much less forgives.

A board meeting was called and all the directors were told they had to come in, even the ones from Wales. This was serious business.

We were sat around the board table and my father proposed my dismissal. One of the board members seconded it and the others agreed.

Even when they put it to the vote, I still thought there was no way they could sack me. But they did - even the directors I thought were on my side voted for the chop. And it was goodbye Val.

Funnily enough, I don't remember them giving any cast-iron reason for my dismissal or citing any particular clause in my contract. It was just a sacking, "you're out", a summary dismissal. Arbitrary and final.

I was dumbstruck: I think I possibly went white. Shock turned to anger as I eyed the other directors who had double-crossed me, betrayed me in the cruellest way imaginable. Weasels and hypocrites, the lot of 'em. It was a stitch-up and they knew it. They knew it because just weeks earlier they'd agreed to send my father that letter urging him to resign, and here they are acceding to a motion from the same man to fire his own flesh and blood. Treachery is not the word for it. I could have strangled each and everyone one of them there and then.

And there's mother and father sat opposite me, stony-faced and implacable. Not a trace of remorse, not a hint of contrition for robbing their own daughter of her livelihood. And what about Victoria? Not even the tiniest regret for the granddaughter I had to provide for?

Fathers don't sack their daughters. It was like The Twilight Zone. Bill will never believe it.

When I told him, he was in shock. We were both furious, but mainly we were sad and quite frankly in disbelief that one's own parents could do such a thing to their own kith and kin. I'd worked hard and extremely well for the company for 12 years and never asked for any special favours despite being the owner's daughter. Twelve years' hard work and a summary dismissal from the father I had worshipped and adored since I was a little girl. Foolishly, I'd put him on that pedestal, but obviously the plinth was rotten from the very start.

If ever there was a case for unfair dismissal, this was it. I got myself a solicitor who prepared a case for an employment tribunal I was sure I would win. My solicitor was meticulous in his preparation and said I had a strong case. I was very confident the judge would rule in our favour.

I got a letter through the post confirming the tribunal date and venue, a building near the old Teesside Gazette offices in town. There was no trepidation yet: my solicitor had done his research and knew his case law alright. I had full confidence in him.

Father offered me a £1,000 out-of-court settlement before the case opened, but I refused because I wanted justice. Besides, there was no way I was accepting a measly offer like that after so many years' hard work. Derisory wasn't even the word. I was taking this the whole way and I was going to win, and he was going to pay me every bit I was due.

One of the older ladies in the office agreed to testify for me, which I thought was very brave knowing what she was up against and the knowledge, surely, that she could surely lose her own job as a result. It was a massive boon for us because she was a nice lady, highly-respected in the company and her husband was a bank manager, which we thought would give her extra clout. Then other staffers said they would take the stand for me which filled me with great hope, as well as gratitude.

Carmel, our nanny, agreed to give evidence because she had proof of father's infidelities. Another staff member, one of the younger ones, had agreed to give evidence for my father, but I think he might have been screwing her.

When we walked into the tribunal and I looked at the old judge, my heart sank. This was 1977 and the old order was still in place. Women were second-class citizens and the younger generation were generally frowned upon and not to be trusted. I knew the judge was on my father's side before he even opened his mouth.

Mother and father walked in looking as cocky as ever and every bit like they knew they were onto a winner. Here I am, sat in an employment tribunal, fighting my own parents against my dismissal from a company owned by my father. It's surreal; it's not normal.

They shot me a look and I shot one back. They had a look of supreme confidence mixed with disgust for the daughter they believed had betrayed them. My confidence was rapidly draining but I put on a brave face and tried to remain strong and calm.

The pair of them just lied their way through the entire tribunal and the judge seemed to buy the whole rot, this steady stream of drivel. He swallowed their bunkum whole.

My father basically shot my character to pieces and told the tribunal that my sacking had been agreed by the whole board because I'd had the gall to ask him to retire. If truth be told, it was the board members who had formally asked my father to resign, but this seemed to go unnoticed, or at least above the judge's head.

And then my mother takes to the stand, points at me and says: "She runs the place like it's hers. She thinks she owns it!"

When I tried to counter this absurd claim, my mother hissed: "She's lying."

How she could know that, or rather allege, I just don't know because you hardly saw her at the company after I got back from America. She'd worked there in the early days, serving in the shop and answering the phones, but after I got back from the States she was never there. I told the judge that I effectively ran the place because my father was always away, but they were basically insinuating that I had designs above my station, on taking the business over, an eye on the big prize. What utter tosh. Complete nonsense.

They said some awful things about me and compared with their barbed insults and character assassinations, we were quite tame and matter-of-fact – perhaps too much so.

I was still reeling from this diatribe when the usher called me to the stand. I took a deep breath and walked past my parents to the witness box. I thought I was doing okay until it all became a bit too much and I started to blubber a bit. I controlled myself very quickly, but the old judge said: "Don't try and fool us with your tears."

Fool you? I'm in bits here!

And then it got really horrible when the tribunal heard every last sordid detail about my father's womanising and adultery. Carmel gave evidence and said my father would often turn up at our house out of the blue and give her washing from this caravan where he used to take one of his floozies for midweek jaunts. She said on oath that he came to the house with other women, but I don't think they believed a word she said. I just think they thought it was too ridiculous to be real.

Carmel was one of the most honest people on the face of the earth, and so was I. But our testimonies were basically dismissed out of hand, rubbished, even mocked. The condescension and suspicion that came our way were totally unwarranted and utterly bizarre.

The old staff lady who agreed to testify for me took to the stand and confirmed my assertion that father was never at work, but I don't think they believed her either. Was there a single witness on behalf of the claimant (me) who could be believed in this room? From the look on the judge's face, I guessed not.

I was cross-examined by my parents' lawyer who did his best to choke me up and suggested that if, as I had alleged, my father was barely there and not pulling his weight, then I, as his daughter and company secretary, should have done something about it before it came to this, rather than dragging it through a costly employment tribunal. But how could I have known I'd be summoned to a board meeting to be sacked by my own father? It was preposterous, but that's what really lost me the tribunal.

The judge concluded: "You were his daughter and a director - you should have known what was going on."

And that was that: we'd lost, and I didn't get a penny. We were gobsmacked 'cos I'd given so much evidence about everything I'd done for the company: the accounts, the phones, the drawing and all the creative stuff. My solicitor was so aghast he halved my fees.

"I can't believe that man was sitting there looking at his own daughter and he could have stopped the proceedings at any time," he said to me with a deep frown.

This was just a week after my mother had come moaning to me about her errant husband who was shagging all her friends and up to God knows what behind her back, yet at the tribunal she stuck to him like you-know-what to a blanket. She was his bosom buddy again, yet just seven days earlier she'd said he needed certifying and called him a whore master!

I always said he was a bastard and mother must have known it, but he was the only bastard she ever had. After all, only a bastard could get on with a woman like her.

The young woman who had spoken up for my father was just protecting her own back and I suppose you can't blame her. She must have been under his thumb. She was the stock-taker, entrusted with a lot of business 'cos we sold a lot of spares, like washing machines, vacuum cleaners and things. But I worked there all hours and I also did the stock-taking, staying behind and going in weekends. None of this was ever acknowledged when I was at the company or at the tribunal.

Those who had spoken up for me went back to the company, but I don't think they lasted very long.

It was a travesty. People were working like mad at that place and he was out with women all day. Alright, he built the place up from nothing, all on his own, but he was also responsible for other directors and members of staff.

I will say this about my father: he was a good businessman and a very savvy operator. He had contacts in America and he merged the company with an outfit in Wales. We had a few Welsh directors on the board who put money into the business, but they both welshed on me.

I'm on the employment scrapheap at 32 and my own parents had seen to it. A sordid turn of events.

Chapter 13

My Girl Victoria

Father thought he could do whatever he wanted, and he did just that - all his life. He must have been born under a lucky star 'cos he was nothing to look at, and he treated people like dirt. Only now did I realise the full extent of his duplicity.

He'd got away with murder for years and people were only too willing to indulge him 'cos he had money and paid people's wages. Money goes a long way in this world, sincerity does not.

I thought he was a saint and then the realisation dawned that he was anything but. I kept my counsel because he was my father and for many years he could do no wrong in my eyes. It was he who told me I looked "lovely pet" on my wedding day when mother didn't want to be there. He was the one who rescued me from my hell in Louisiana, and it was father who had visited me every day in hospital when I had that horrible first childbirth. Mother never did.

But I realised that the man and the father figure he projected to the world was all a sham, and that the only person he really cared about was himself.

Mother's problem had nothing to do with deceit and hypocrisy — quite the opposite, in fact. She was abrupt in the extreme; she'd say whatever she liked to people and wouldn't give a damn if she hurt anybody's feelings.

After the tribunal, I barred them from seeing or contacting Victoria. I couldn't let them see my child after what they had done to me. They had thought nothing of her future when they sacked me and to my mind they had no right to any sort of grandparental privilege.

One day, Carmel went to pick Victoria up from infants' school, but my parents had already been at the gates. They were waiting for Victoria, who was confused and scared. Her grandparents were trying to take her out of school, but where on earth were they planning to take her?

She went to her teacher and said: "My grandma and grandad are at the gate and I'm not allowed to see them."

Her teacher went out to see my parents and told them to leave. I don't know what their response was, but she got them to go. When she got home, Victoria was almost in tears.

"Mam, grandma and grandad were at the gate," she said.

I got in touch with my solicitor and he wrote them a letter warning them not to go near her again. Not long afterwards, Carmel said she saw my mother drive slowly past the house looking in, no doubt hoping that Victoria was playing outside.

I still have no idea what they were up to. I don't think they wanted to abduct her, but what did they think they could possibly achieve through intimidating my daughter in this way? Did they want her? Or did they just want to get at me?

I was so proud of my daughter for telling the teacher that she wasn't allowed to see them. Even at her tender age, she knew what they had done to me and why they weren't allowed to see her.

Victoria was a delicate flower, far from ready to deal with adult strife. She was an artistic child who loved music and bought albums from the age of eight. Her first 'grown-up' album was something called Parallel Lines by Blondie, and she never missed Top of the Pops. She also shared my love of musicals, especially the Liza Minnelli ones. She was the typical only child, a bit highly-strung, but we never spoiled her. If she asked for something like a racing bike, I'd say: "If you do well at the end of term, you'll get one."

If she spent her pocket money before the week was out and came back for more, I'd say: "No, you've got to learn how to budget."

She left infants' school and moved up to Mill Hill Juniors, a private school which was very Dickensian; an old-fashioned sort of place but the teachers were lovely. Victoria was clever like me and a very creative child. She got 100 per cent for French and was brilliant at English – she'd obviously inherited the linguistic genes. She was no good at maths, but she was a strong speller and her grammar was impeccable.

She got viral meningitis at 10 years old and was taken into hospital where they had to do a lumber puncture to get the fluid off her spine. She was in the old West Lane Hospital in Middlesbrough and it was the school holidays, when she should have been out playing with friends and enjoying the summer break.

We had to put gowns and masks on when we went in to see her because it was contagious and if we brought toys in, we couldn't take them back with us. When I rang up the night after she'd been taken in, they said the liquid in her spine was a strange colour.

"So what does that mean?" I said.

"It means you've got a very ill child, Mrs Yare."

She was in hospital for a week and it was even scarier than when she had the nappy rash as a baby because we knew meningitis was a killer. I say to her now: "That's why you're not the full shilling."

I mean, she's crackers and a bit dizzy, bless her. She's blonde, after all.

Just before she went to high school, Carmel, our nanny, left to go look after her sister's children in Spain, but we made enough time for Victoria as well as bringing in a double wage. Carmel had been a wonderful nanny and gave us six years' great service.

Victoria moved up to Kings Manor in Acklam, a secondary school and listed building with a fabulous wooden staircase and beautiful interior. It was a state school – the private fees were too much for us.

She was in the school play every year and once played a 1920's Charleston floozie with a feather boa and bobbed hair. She joined Middlesbrough Junior Little Theatre. She was very theatrical, like me, and a very good dancer: she did ballet and tap, and disco dancing. She was a natural and won medals.

She had loads of friends and lots of boyfriends: a very popular child in every respect. If truth be told, she was a little sod from the age of 10 to the start of her college years. She was a proper girl: hormonal, fickle, tetchy. There were so many boyfriends that when they rang up I'd say: "Which one are you?"

Victoria was one of those who always stood up for the underdogs and those poor kids living with disabilities. She brought them home to us and they were all lovely children. One girl had an abnormally wide leg; another girl was crippled with arthritis at just 13 years old. There was another with spina bifida who we just loved.

Victoria got a few O' Levels and did well in English, but she under-achieved like me. She was turning into a fine young thespian but packed it in after she left school and got a Saturday job at the Fresh & Fruity food shop in Acklam. She also had three babysitting jobs and worked in the café at Littlewoods.

She never really trusted her grandparents again after the incident at the school gates and particularly mistrusted my father. It was unforgiveable of them to mess around with her head at such a tender age when she's just finding her feet in the world and going through all these changes. They made her a pawn in our fight. It was disgraceful because our falling-out had nothing to do with her, but mother and father only ever thought of themselves.

I started childminding and absolutely loved it. I'd been a nanny back in the 60s, so for me it was easy-peasy. I'd always been good with kids.

It was around the same time we got our first dogs. One of them was a scruffy mongrel called Smokey who was just gorgeous, like one of those little Disney dogs. We got him from a rescue centre which had taken him in after his owners moved to Norway, put him in kennels for six months and never came back. He took ill when he was 13 and we had to have him put down.

We also got a rescue whippet called Toby who'd been thrown out of a car when his owners moved home. Every time we put Toby in the car to go to the vet's, he used to pee all over me 'cos he thought he was going to be thrown out. The poor little thing was petrified.

Toby took quite a shine to the chickens we kept in a coop behind the garage, eyeing them like a mega-bucket of KFC chicken nuggets. He looked like a fox to them and they'd go berserk every time he went past. He never killed any of them, but I once found him with his paw on one of the chicken's backsides, plucking all the feathers out of its rear end. The chicken ended up with a very raw posterior.

Another time, I walked into the chicken coop to feed them and I was reading a letter. I forgot to shut the door. Toby got in and all hell broke loose. The chickens got out. They were going crazy. They were all over the fence, the garden, and in my hair.

We kept the chickens for fresh eggs and to show the children I was looking after 'cos they were fascinated by them. I set up the

Middlesbrough Childminding group which was so successful that Look North, the regional news programme, sent out a reporter to interview me at my home. I sang 'Hickory, Dickory, Dock' with the children live on TV. I acted out the nursery rhyme and it made a nice little news feature. Mike Neville was presenting.

The first lot of chickens had to go because they got some kind of disease which made their feathers fall out. We got another six pullets, but they had to go too after I went back out to work. I'd been training to be a health-and-safety officer at Stockton Billingham College and I passed with flying colours.

Victoria left school and went to the same college to study elderly care. She met a guy called Richard at a nightclub. He would eventually become her husband.

She got her carer's certificate and found a job at an old people's home in North Ormesby, where she became assistant manager because she was so good at her job. She was highly popular with the residents and when one of the elderly ladies – a woman called Norma, in her late 60s – got married, she asked Victoria to be a bridesmaid.

Norma had met her husband-to-be, a gentleman of about the same age, in the local pub where nursing staff used to take the residents for a sing-along and get-together on a Saturday night. Their marriage was all over the papers and on Look North.

Victoria and Richard courted for three years, then got married at St Mary's Church in Acklam in October 1990. She was just 20 years old.

Bill walked her down the aisle, but he didn't look right. He seemed very nervous. When they got to the bottom of the aisle, I noticed his feet going wobbly.

I thought: "What the hell is he doing, showing me up?"

And the next thing he's collapsed on the floor, in a screaming heap. Down like a lead weight. He landed head-first on Victoria's veil. She couldn't move, not even her head, and she's screaming: "Oh no, me dad! Me dad!"

One of the wedding guests, Mrs Onions, was a 100-year-old lady from the care home who turned up in a wheelchair.

"Does he want my chair?" said Mrs Onions, who had the congregation crying with laughter despite the obvious concern for Bill.

The guests were bemused. The vicar was having kittens. Bill was out for the count. It was like something off 'You've Been Framed', except we didn't have a video camera to record it.

A friend of ours, a police sergeant called John who had done first aid, was out of his pew like a shot and came down to the front. He crouched down and started working on Bill, loosened his tie. Sweat was pouring from Bill's forehead like a little waterfall. He wasn't moving.

John got him to sit up, but he looked terrible. He'd only been out for a minute, but he was in no fit state to give Victoria away. His brother, Ray, had to step in and do the honours.

Bill came round in time for the photos and wedding reception at the Masonic Hall in Middlesbrough, but I was worried that he wouldn't be able to deliver his speech. I looked over at him with something approaching mild panic as he stood up to give his toast.

"Ladies and gentlemen," he said, "I'm okay now." And everybody cheered.

He did the speech fine. He was determined to see it through for Victoria, a daddy's girl if ever there was one. He adored her. Everyone loved her. She was always good with people and always wanted to help those less fortunate than herself.

After the reception we went to the care home to show the residents Victoria in her wedding dress. The old ladies were all crying. I was so proud - she was a natural with the old folks.

We got the wedding photos back and I noticed Bill's jacket was fastened on the wrong button when he was bringing Victoria down the aisle. Poor lad was as nervous as a kitten.

Victoria left the old people's home to go work as a mentor and care assistant for teenage children with mental-health problems at the Roseberry Centre in the grounds of St Luke's Hospital in Middlesbrough. She was brilliant with those kids: she used to cook with them, paint with them, take them to the shops, take them camping. She was one of the few there who actually did things with the kids and taught them life skills.

One day at the centre, which by then had moved to the West Lane Hospital, she walked into the communal lounge and found a lad with a noose around his neck, hanging from a rope. She got him down, a few minutes from death.

At the old Roseberry Centre, she was the one who used to chase the children, particularly the lads, who'd done a runner across the fields. She used to chase them and rugby-tackle them. She was very fit and when they knew it was her running after them, they'd just stop running because they knew they couldn't outrun her. She outran her grandparents too – they barely saw her again after the incident at the school gates.

Chapter 14

The Rottweiler

The fall-out with my parents would never heal and quite frankly our separation was probably the best outcome for both parties. Our relationship was irreconcilable, fractured beyond repair.

My faith in humanity had been tested to breaking point and I lost trust in people. How can you trust people when your own parents get you sacked from a job you love and then go hunting for your daughter at the school gates?

I tried my best to put it out of my mind and over the next few years I concentrated on my new career, my family and my dogs. We just adored Ben, our gorgeous Border Collie, and we minded Victoria's two adorable Border Terriers when she was at work.

We felt like we were finally putting everything behind us and then Victoria got divorced. It wasn't Richard's fault, nor Victoria's. There were just irreconcilable differences which I don't really want to go into and they decided it was best to part ways.

Bill and I couldn't have been more pleased when Victoria chose Richard as her husband. He was a lovely lad and a good worker with a solid job and an even temper. He was, in short, everything you could ever wish for in a son-in-law. We thought they would live happily ever after, but things never turn out as you expect.

I was starting to get a bit down again, but then along came a man who not only kick-started a long and fulfilling career, but also restored my faith in mankind. His name was Jack Youdale, a lovely fellow who was to become the most inspirational person in my life.

Jack - whose daughter was 'Jet' from The Gladiators TV show - was an ex-ICI worker who had started working in a Government training programme under the old YTS scheme. The Government set up these training centres all over the country where people would learn teaching and negotiation skills to get their training certificates. Jack ran a couple of couple of Health and Safety half-day courses at the Cleveland Accredited Training Centre where we worked. I told him I was really interested in health and safety and that's where it all started.

My boss asked me to write a half-day H&S course and I astounded her by discussing interaction and including exercises within the course. As good as Jack was, he just used to talk to the candidates, but I set out a blueprint for making the courses more dynamic, much livelier and getting the candidates to interact more. My role was basically to train the trainers.

When I started doing health and safety, the training accounted for five per cent of the company's revenue. By the time I'd left, it had shot up to 85 per cent. I introduced new qualifications and I was asked to pilot some in 1992 for national bodies such as the Institute of Occupational Safety and Health (IOSH). I put hundreds of candidates through and they all got nationally-recognised certificates with my name on.

My boss paid for me to go to college to gain the NEBOSH qualification - that's National Examining Board of Occupational Health & Safety, in case you were wondering. I'd finally got letters after my name: I always had, but up until now the only acronym I could call my own was 'TTS', and that, if you were wondering, is short for 'Too much of a Trusting Soul'.

I ended up going self-employed as a freelance health-and-safety consultant. It was a job I would never leave. I loved it with a passion.

Jack, a kind and gentle man and my great mentor, died a year ago, in his 90s. He was the catalyst for me at a time when I needed someone to trust. He was honest to a fault and a very clever man, well into his astronomy and a renowned authority on the subject. He was part of an astronomical society and it was he who persuaded people in the right places to build the Wynyard Planetarium and Observatory in Stockton-on-Tees, which is now a very popular attraction.

My freelance work meant I could put even more distance between me and my parents. I soon earned a reputation as a health-and-safety "Rottweiler" – my new nickname among those to whom I laid down the law. If they stuck by the rules, they would get to know the kind and caring Val Yare. But if they stepped out of line and flouted the rules, I'd give 'em both barrels. Without doubt, many of them were frightened of me, hence the nickname. They learnt to do as they were told, or else.

Being self-employed was ideal for me because of the flexible working hours and the days off, but I had a ferocious work ethic. Because of my forthright style, I never took any prisoners and some of them didn't like being told what to do. It gets their back up, you see. They think the rules are stupid and there to be dodged. They think they are unfair. They are wrong.

"What is this bureaucracy all about?" they would say.

And I'd reply: "It's the law – don't shoot the messenger."

This has always been my way and you can either like it or lump it. What you see is what you get, but some people seem frightened by straight-talking.

I put a big premium on honesty. I think it started with Jim and then my father, two liars of the highest order who ought never to have roamed God's clean earth. I took Jim at face value and he turned out to be one of the Devil's own. I worshipped my father and then he too took me to the depths of hell. Two people who, at one time, I loved the most, were nothing but compulsive twisters of the truth. They were no-good charlatans, inside-out characters who got by on a modicum of charm and a complete lack of scruple.

To this day, I cannot stand liars, I really can't. It really needles me. Now, if somebody lies to me, that's it. We never speak again. At one time I'd have given them a second chance, but not anymore. I bring people up on it all the time.

"What have you just said? I'll say. "That's not true!"

And it knocks them for six. They don't know how to handle it.

Once, I'd heard that somebody at work had said something about me and I waited for her to come in.

"I need a word with you," I said. "If you want to say anything to me, you say it to my face."

Her mouth dropped wide open.

That's what I became post-Jim, and that's how I am now. I don't take any crap; I don't suffer fools. I had, and still have, no time for false and superficial people. I give them short shrift and tell them where to go. They know not to mess.

Throughout my years in health and safety, there have been people who've challenged me and refused to obey the rules out of sheer obstinacy. You'd tell them something and they'd go: "Oh, this is bloody stupid."

And that of course was their misfortune. They soon learned that disobedience was a foolish move.

Some were just daft or lazy, or both. One day a guy climbed to the top of a ladder without a hard hat on and I went berserk. I was delivering a training course on the first floor of this building when this ladder came up and rested just outside the window. Then up pops this guy's head without any protection on. I saw red and went into Rottweiler mode.

"You haven't got a hard hat on!" I snapped as I opened the window and looked down on his gormless face. He was startled.

"It's down there," he said, pointing at the ground.

"Well that's a lot of bloody good, isn't it, if you fall and break your skull?!"

He just looked at me kind of horrified and scuttled back down the ladder.

I went on construction sites and stuck it to the brickies and foremen who maybe sniggered at first at the sight of this waif-like young lady who broadly spoke the Queen's English, but they soon learnt the error of their ways. If they displeased me, I'd tear into them.

I went into big businesses and top chain restaurants and laid down the law until they didn't dare step out of line. Hard as nails.

There were some who would try to belittle me and show who was boss 'cos they were big shots and I was a little woman, but they too soon learnt I was no shrinking violet.

Once, I had a class full of people on a course for organisations looking to recruit university graduates for major companies when I got my first taste of misogynism in the workplace. I was trying to explain to the heads of these recruitment firms how they must vet the placements for health and safety before they put the students in. One guy rolled his eyes and said snootily: "We deal with blue-chip companies."

He was basically telling me that he and his company were above all this. He was being really clever to the point of sheer rudeness. Every time I passed a hand-out around the group, he would smirk and say: "Thanks flower."

The hairs on the back of my neck bristled and I felt myself raging. The women in the class were looking at me and could see I wasn't happy. I passed some more hand-outs around the class and this cretin was smirking again.

"Thanks flower," he repeated.

"You're ok, cock," I replied.

I'd cut him down in three words. The women were trying to keep a straight face, but I think a few sniggers broke out.

Others, mainly males, used industrial language to try to intimidate and embarrass me, but if they thought a few profanities would cow me, they were badly mistaken. One bloke thought he was being ever so clever when, during a training session, he kept effing and blinding.

"I really don't mind you swearing," I said. "If you swear, that's fine with me, but I think you need to have some respect for people in this class, especially the ladies."

He was speechless. Outgunned. And he didn't swear anymore after that. In fact, he was quite polite. You've just got to know how to deal with these people. Play them at their own game; call their bluff. I was no man-hating feminist: I generally love men. But I would never let them belittle or talk down to me, no way. Not after what I'd been through with Jim and my father.

There was this other guy at the Boulby Potash mines who tried it on and I took him to the cleaners. I was there to check they were complying with the new European health-and-safety regulations, which had just come into place. This guy, called Jack, was stewing over a motor that had gone wrong and I tried to offer some advice, but he dismissed it out of hand.

"You won't understand because you're a woman," he said.

I didn't get angry - just diagnosed the problem within seconds.

"It sounds to me like the carbon brushes have gone," I replied.

He was gobsmacked.

At the end of the lesson, he said he'd like to say something and I thought: "Oh, here we go."

"I'd like to say I've learnt more in half a day with you than I did on a full-week course," he said.

Ye gods! I was stunned.

The HR officer took me to one side afterwards and said: "I hear you put Jack in his place there."

I was flattered, but I already knew I was good because people kept recommending me and I always went over and above what was required.

I was very happy at work and Bill got a new job at Teesside University as the refectory storekeeper, which he enjoyed despite no holiday pay. We were content, we were doing okay financially, and then Victoria became seriously ill.

She'd been struggling to breathe and couldn't even walk properly. Her co-ordination went haywire and she couldn't even get out of bed. We were all deeply confused as to what it might be, and it was all the more frightening because she was living on her own following the divorce.

She rang me one night and said: "Mam, can I come and stay with you 'cos I'm not well at all. I can hardly breathe."

I took her to an emergency clinic and they referred her to Middlesbrough General Hospital who sent her to James Cook Hospital.

She had X-rays but they didn't know what was wrong with her. They put her on a drip and filled her full of steroids. She had to have her lungs drained because they were full of fluid. They said they thought she might have a rare lung cancer, then they thought she may have lupus. We were scared stiff.

Victoria had to have all her rings cut off because her fingers had swelled up. This thing she had, whatever it was, was even worse than the meningitis we thought might kill her as a child. The doctors were very concerned and the prognosis was bleak. It seemed for all the world that she was dying.

The poor thing was laid in bed with her face all grey and lifeless and all me and Bill could do was hold her hand and tell her we loved her. We were convinced she was going to die. She was in so much pain it made us cry. They did loads of tests but they all came back inconclusive. We were completely baffled.

I suspected, but couldn't be sure, that the illness had been brought on by her work at the mental-health unit at St Luke's. The day before she took ill, she had to restrain an unruly boy for nearly five hours because she and the other staff weren't allowed to give him an injection to sedate him until the doctor arrived to give permission. Victoria and a few of her colleagues had to pin the boy down and I just wondered if being in that position for so long had led to her illness.

She was in hospital for weeks and didn't get any better. It was touch and go. Then one night, as she was laid in bed, she found herself talking to somebody and saying: "Please don't let me die, I'm too young. If you let me live, I'll follow you for the rest of my life."

Victoria, like us, wasn't a believer and had never been in touch with God. We were never church-going people and agnostic at best. Except for Christenings, marriages and funerals, we'd never set foot inside a church for years. And here's Victoria, in a hospital bed, asking for deliverance from on high. She got it, thank God.

Her recovery was slow at first, but then, after about three weeks, she began to regain her strength and was finally able to get out of bed and start walking around the ward and down the corridors. It was like a miracle and, unbeknown to us, she pledged her life to Christ from then on.

They never really found out what was wrong with her. They just said it was something pulmonary and now she'd got ME. Oh, whoopee.

They just filled her full of steroids and sent her home, which was a huge relief for us 'cos now she's out of the woods, but she was chronically fatigued all the time. Her bosses at the mental-health unit said there was no way she could do nights anymore with ME and put her on a day shift. Her mind and body must have been shot to bits. We despaired and wondered how much more we could take.

Victoria loved her job working with young people, but she was totally burnt out. It was viral ME which can come and go, but she never did go back on nights. She ended up leaving the hospital and going for a job with the energy firm Npower.

The one thing that sustained Victoria was her new-found belief. It was a leap of faith and she hasn't looked back since.

As soon as she got out of hospital she enrolled on an Alpha course, like an induction for prospective Christians who are on the cusp of faith but need that extra bit of teaching and reassurance before they commit. Victoria had absolutely no doubt she'd found her true path in life.

Of course, we had no idea she'd converted, and when she got out of hospital we asked her to stay with us 'cos she was on her own and we wanted to keep an eye on her.

One evening we were waiting for her to come home from a night out when she phoned us about 10 o'clock.

"Just to let you know I won't be long," She said.

"Where are you?" I said.

"Oh, I won't be long."

I turned to Bill and said she must be in the pub or something, but when she got home she said: "Mam and dad, I've got something to tell you."

I thought: "My God, what has happened?"

"Oh, I've become a Christian," she said.

"Oh, is that all?"

We'd noticed the change in her after she'd got out of hospital, but we weren't quite sure what had brought it on, maybe just the relief of getting out alive. We didn't ask questions 'cos we were just so relieved she was still with us.

The transformation was remarkable: she was so much happier and at ease with herself. She was no longer so head-strong and she rediscovered a trust in people. She looked outside herself and said she was beginning to see things she didn't see before, like birds and flowers and pretty colours.

Now she'd told us she'd become a Christian, it all made sense, not that we were in any way inclined towards the teachings of the church. Bill was bordering on atheist.

She told us it was all down to the Alpha course and Jesus. She said it put everything into perspective. She'd been going to this church and it had changed her life completely. She said it was all about putting others before yourself.

We saw this startling transformation in our daughter and though we were non-believers, we were more than content for her to take this leap if it meant she was happy. But at the same time, we were worried it might be some sort of cult she'd got herself into and fretted endlessly.

And then she starts talking to us about going along to the Alpha Supper. Goodness me.

The Alpha Supper was apparently the first step to becoming a Christian, but we imagined strange people with strange names who hugged and kissed a lot.

Victoria knew we were deeply sceptical and worried about what she was getting into, but she was persistent.

"There's an Alpha course running," She said excitedly. "Would you like to come to the Alpha Supper? I just want you to meet my friends."

Bill looked at me and shook his head. This was totally out of our comfort zone. We weren't Christian people. We were extremely dubious, but we decided to go along anyway, just to make sure it wasn't a cult.

Well, we needn't have been so sceptical. We walked into this room and I was surrounded by love. The supper was lovely and I'd never met so many nice people in one place in all my life.

I said to Bill: "Shall we go on the course?"

He still looked doubtful but shrugged his shoulders.

I said to Victoria: "We're going on the course, but we're not going to become Christians."

"Aye, OK mam," She said, with a wry smile. She knew we'd see the light.

Chapter 15

Salvation

Victoria was surely onto something, though we didn't know quite what yet. I thought if she's so happy, then maybe I could be too. And what's wrong with that?

She'd found a contentedness and an inner peace which beguiled us. I thought she must know something we don't because she's walking around like she's on Cloud Nine all the time.

She'd been going to this church called Jubilee and worship was held at a school hall in Middlesbrough. According to Victoria, there were hundreds of people there every Sunday and the atmosphere was incredible. There was singing, dancing, clapping and the playing of instruments, nothing like the stuffy atmosphere of your average Anglican church. You could have fun and make friends, she said.

There was no sitting on pews, no fire and brimstone. It was evangelical, New Testament, easy-going, she assured me.

But Bill and I had never been anywhere near God. There was nobody more sceptical than me (except Bill), but we were intrigued. We were curious.

We decided to go on the Alpha course and again we were struck by the sheer warmth of the people and the general loveliness of it all. They were so welcoming and non-judgemental. It was like nothing we'd ever experienced before.

The Alpha course was presented by a pastor called Jeremy, a lovely bloke who would become a great friend. We asked hundreds of questions, the usual questions that atheists, agnostics and sceptics tend to ask: Is this a cultish practice in any way? Might we get brainwashed? If there is a god, why do babies die? Why are there wars? Why is there so much suffering in the world? What is this thing you call 'charismatic renewal'? What's this so-called Restoration Movement? Do we have to pray in tongues? And do we have to have our heads dunked?

125

I felt myself changing but I couldn't bring myself to make the leap. I'd always believed there was a god, but I never believed that Jesus was the son of God. I always thought he was a prophet.

The course lasted 10 weeks and by the end of it all, you have what they call an 'Away Day'. It's proper name is The Holy Spirit Day, but they must have thought that might frighten people off, so they renamed it the Away Day. On our Away Day, we went to a hotel for lunch instead of the usual church buffet.

After lunch, Jeremy gave a sermon about the Jews' exodus from Egypt and their flight across the wilderness, where they lived in tabernacles, or tents, on their way to the Promised Land. The Jews celebrated the Tabernacle every year thereafter, to pray for water and crops.

"One year, this guy called Jesus came along and spoilt the day," said Jeremy.

"He walked up and said, 'Those who are thirsty, come to *me* and drink'. Those who believe will have rivers of water flowing through them.'" (John: Chapter 7, Verses 37 and 38).

I didn't realise how thirsty I'd been, not even during the drought in Louisiana when I was slurping in the raindrops and getting laughed at. But after hearing Jeremy recite that passage from the bible, I knew I would never thirst again.

In the church, 'coming forward', or 'stepping forward', is a sign that you're ready to commit and offer your life to Christ. I didn't go forward during the sermon, but I was really close.

Somebody on the other side of the room said: "There's somebody over there who's not moving, but they want to move."

She meant me.

"Hmm," I thought, still sceptical.

Jed, another church elder, said: "There's somebody who wants to come forward and God is saying to you, 'Who do you think was there for you through all your bad times?'"

Well, no-one actually. My father, but he proved to be a total waste of time.

I asked Julie, our table leader, to take me forward, and that was it. I was saved.

Bill stayed rooted to the spot. He just couldn't get his head around the resurrection. He thought it was scientifically and biologically impossible.

Victoria was baptised in the River Swale at Richmond. We took picnics and watched with great excitement as her friend and her husband, who were both members of Jubilee, lead her down to the bottom of the bank. They waded into the river and they totally submerged her in the freezing water. The look of pure elation on her face when she re-emerged was something I'll never forget. It was like she'd been re-born.

Just after they got out of the river and climbed back up the bank, the heavens opened and we all got drenched. We ran back to the car sopping wet, but Victoria was ecstatic.

We had to eat our picnic in the car. Others got baptised on the same day and they all gave their testimonies on the river bank, explaining how they had found God before they went into the river. We drove home and I just knew in my heart that I would take the plunge.

I got baptised at Oakwood Church in Eaglescliffe, Stockton-on-Tees, which we hired for the day because Jubilee didn't have a pool back then. Jed and Victoria led me down into the cross-shaped pool and all the church members were at poolside with beaming smiles. There were about four of us getting baptised that day. The trepidation was immense, but I was so excited.

I had to give my testimony before I was baptised, and just before I was submerged I told Victoria: "I don't like water, so don't hold me down too long."

Everyone laughed.

Jed and Victoria placed their hands on the top of my head, then eased me down. Suddenly I was submerged. For the first time in my life, I wasn't afraid in the water, and I resurfaced a new woman.

Everybody was clapping and yelling when I got out of the pool. It was the happiest day of my life. I felt like I was walking on air. For the rest of the day, I felt like I was floating six feet above the ground. I was in my mid-fifties and felt like a teenage girl all of a sudden.

We persuaded Bill to do another Alpha course, but still he wouldn't commit. The resurrection was still bothering him.

When you get baptised, you receive the Holy Spirit. But there's a big difference between receiving the Holy Spirit and being *filled* with the Holy Spirit. Once you allow the Holy Spirit inside you, it's an entirely different ball game, because then you know that you're one with God and all your doubts just disappear. Your questions go out of the window because there are no more questions to answer. You know you've found Him.

And that's when I knew I would never be alone, no matter what happened. We'd had some pretty awful things happen to us, but God never said things would be easy and at least you knew He was there with you. That's the difference and, believe me, it does help.

Things are bound to go wrong at times with or without Jesus, because God gave man free will. It's not God, but man, that causes the problems.

When the Holy Spirit gets inside you, the feeling you have inside is like a river about to burst its banks. The Spirit just explodes out of you and you end up jabbering away in a language that is totally alien to you. Sometimes you can't stop laughing.

We pray in tongues because speaking through the lips in our own language is simply not enough to express the power of the Holy Spirit and our praise to God. He gives many gifts and one of them is the gift of tongues.

It wouldn't make any sense to non-believers, and to be honest when I first heard people praying in tongues it sounded like gobbledegook, but in church you have interpreters who will pass on this message from God, via the receiver, for someone else, because sometimes you 'get a tongue' and it means nothing to you. It's usually interpreted in English, but also in Farsi and Tigrinyan, an Afro/Asiatic language. Ours is a modern church and we have people of many different nationalities: Iranians, Iraqis, Afghans, Nigerians, Ethiopians, South Africans. And more.

When we're praying 'in the Spirit', the words of the Holy Spirit just flow through us. It's irresistible, it's intoxicating - and it's real. It's what the disciples did when the Holy Spirit came upon them at The Pentecost. When the Spirit blew in, they could see fire and they all started praying in tongues.

After the Resurrection, Jesus said to the Apostles: "I will leave my Holy Spirit within you, for you to go to the ends of the earth and spread my Gospel."

I used to think it was blind faith, but it wasn't that at all. I had never been so convinced about anything in my life, and I knew God would never let me down. My Father God is with me every hour of the day.

When I was on the Alpha course, I got talking to a lady, a devout Catholic who lived across the way from us, and I told her I didn't really understand it all.

"You know what," I said, "I don't understand. They say Jesus died for me, but how could he die for me? I wasn't born then."

"I don't know," she said, and that was the end of the conversation.

But that is the crux of Christianity: Jesus did die for us. I know that now. He was the sacrificial lamb, so that we could be close to God.

One day, a colleague of mine, a Catholic, said to me: "You won't believe what somebody called you the other day."

"What?"

"A born-again Christian."

"Yes, that's right; it's in the Bible," I said.

She thought I'd be offended, but I wasn't in the slightest. As far as I was concerned, it didn't matter *when* I found Him; I was just glad that I had, because I knew I'd never be the same again.

One day, a few years later, we had some very bad news in the family and the following Sunday, Bill said: "I think I'll come to church with you today."

He started coming every Sunday from then on, and eventually gave himself to Christ. Out of bad, God brought him to Christ. God always has a plan for you. I honestly believe that he lets things happen for a reason. He never gives you anything you can't handle, but you definitely learn from it and you become stronger. He is always there with you through the good and the bad.

Christians always tell you never to break the bread and drink the wine if you're not one of the faithful, because it's Christ's body and blood. For that reason, Bill never touched the communal wine until he saw the light. He still came to church with us, but he wouldn't step forward.

Then one day he said: "Can I have some bread and wine?"

He came forward and I jumped six feet in the air.

Bill looked at me and said: "Don't make a fuss."

I went looking for the pastors, shouting: "Jeremy! Raj! Jeremy!"

It's a fantastic feeling when you know someone who comes to Jesus and we praise The Lord for the blessing. There's a party in heaven too.

One night, a few weeks later, Bill got filled with the Holy Spirit. He was walking around the room as if his feet weren't touching the floor, grinning from ear to ear. It did my head in.

He'd finally taken the step. All three of us had gone from heathens to true believers in the blink of an eye. And to think it all started in a hospital bed.

Chapter 16

Undesirables

My parents had disappeared into the ether as far as I was concerned. Just a distant, unhappy memory.

I was too busy with work and my family to worry about them and I was getting help for the cat phobia - particularly the ginger ones.

Then one Christmas I went to my nana's to give her a present and my mother and father arrived while I was there. I was sat in the kitchen and my father came in with Elsie, my nana's sister.

"Oh, hello," he said. "You look smart."

"I always do," I replied.

Father left the room and went into the lounge with Elsie.

That left me and my mother sat around the kitchen table with my nana. Mother asked me how Victoria was.

"Fine; she's at college now," I said.

She seemed a little pensive, as if she wanted to tell me something.

"It shouldn't be like this," she said.

"Well, you shouldn't have such a bastard of a husband then, and it wouldn't be," I shot back.

She was in shock; she looked like she was about to have a fit. She said she needed her tablets. And she got some out of her handbag and swallowed them.

When my parents got up to go, I stayed where I was. My mother looked a bit groggy. Elsie went to the door with them. Apparently, my mother was sobbing.

I said to Elsie: "Oh, he'll have a nice Christmas then, won't he?"

It was the last time I saw him.

Time passes so quickly. When I heard my father had died, alone, in a nursing home in Yarm, I couldn't believe it had been so many years since I had last seen him.

He must have been at least 80, but in truth I'd forgotten how old he was. He'd not been a well man for some time. He had a dicky heart and several other illnesses, but I can't be sure what killed him in the end 'cos I never asked.

I used to work with somebody whose sister worked in the home where my father spent his final days. My friend's sister told her that on the day he died, the nursing home rang my mother and said: "We think you should come because we don't think he's going to last the night."

"Oh, I can't come now," she said. "The weather's too bad."

I'm pleased he died on his own. Mother must have loathed him after finding out about the affairs, but in truth they were always an odd couple. I've said it before: he was a bastard, but the only bastard she had.

Had there ever been true affection between my mother and father? A difficult question and hard to tell in the early days because I was too young and I was always frightened of them. They were comfortable with each other, that's for sure. But love? Not sure about that. I don't think either of them were capable of loving anyone but themselves.

I didn't feel anything when I heard father had died and I didn't go to his funeral. I'd barely seen him since he fired me 25 years earlier. I'm not a hypocrite: just because somebody dies, it doesn't mean they sprout wings and become an angel all of a sudden. You only go to funerals out of respect and I certainly didn't respect him. I don't even know where he was laid to rest and I've neve bothered enquiring. I presume it was at the crematorium in Middlesbrough, but I couldn't have cared less.

He'd had a few heart attacks over the years. Back in the 70s, when Victoria was about three, he was diagnosed with a leaking valve and had to go in for major heart surgery to have an artificial valve fitted. He had the operation in Shotley Bridge Hospital and I'd ring up saying: "How's daddy?"

But I really didn't care; it was just a duty that I did.

I suppose his heart must have given out eventually, but I have no idea when he was taken into the care home and I didn't have the foggiest about the deterioration in his health.

It was my great-aunt Rose, on my mother's side, who rang to tell me he'd passed away.

"I've got some bad news for you, Valerie," she said.

"Oh, what bad news? What's happened?"

"Your father's died."

"Oh, right," I said.

She thought it was bad news, but in truth, it was just news.

When she put the phone down, I said to Bill: "My father's died."

"Are you alright?" he said.

"I'm absolutely fine."

If you don't like somebody in life, you won't like them in death either. If you're nasty in life, it doesn't change the person you were just because you've died. And besides, father was always destined for the other place. He was just a whore master.

I have no idea how mother coped in widowhood - probably very well. She ended up living alone in a bungalow in Yarm, where they had moved some years earlier.

It was years before I saw her again, but there was no reconciliation. It was at the funeral of one of my friend's sisters, and it was the same story all over again: utter indifference and not a shred of affection.

I was with Bill and Victoria at the crematorium and we were just leaving the service when I saw a woman who looked a bit like my mother, but I couldn't be sure because it had been years since I'd last seen her.

I turned to my uncle and said: "Is that my mother over there?"

"Yeah, that's your mother."

So I went up to her and said: "This is Victoria."

Mother looked at her and said: "Oh my, you are beautiful."

And then she started talking about her ailments again, mainly the bad knees.

Victoria had seen her once or twice over the past 20 years - once in an outpatients' department when she took a neighbour for a hospital appointment. Apparently, it wasn't a joyous reunion and Victoria hadn't had anything to do with her since the falling-out over two decades earlier.

Still, she sent my mother a sympathy card when my father died, even though Victoria hated my father in the end. In this respect, I think Victoria deserved a little bit more than "Oh you are beautiful" and bad knee joints.

I didn't mind mother disliking me, but I could not accept this ambivalence towards her own granddaughter who, after all, had done nothing wrong and was in no way involved in this set-to that they had brought about.

But I suppose as far as mother was concerned, Victoria was guilty by association, just the next one in the line of undesirables. And therefore unworthy of the slightest consideration. God give me strength.

I think deep down she loved her granddaughter, but I made sure she wasn't going to hurt her like she hurt me.

One day, years later, I went for lunch with a colleague at The Marton Hotel & Country Club in Middlesbrough and there was mother. An old woman in every sense and I didn't know it was her until she opened her mouth.

She clearly didn't recognise me and spoke only to my colleague at the table where we were sat. As she walked out, mother smiled at my colleague but ignored me. I looked at her, but there was no recognition. I got up from the table and followed her out, because I felt I had to make myself known.

I walked up to her and said: "Are you Vi?"

"Yes."

"I'm your daughter."

"Really?"

And then she starts telling me about her bad knees.

"Never mind your bad knees," I thought. "Your eyesight can't be that good if you don't know who I am."

There was just no bond. I felt nothing. We were complete strangers.

I have to admit: it saddened me that she didn't recognise me. And all she wanted to do was talk about herself and her bad knees.

"What are you doing now?" She said.

"Health and safety."

"Oh yeah, my sister told me."

Cue a very long, awkward silence.

Then she says: "How's Victoria?"

"Fine."

"Who are you with?"

"A colleague."

She didn't ask after Bill – he was beyond the pale. They never got on.

The week after our somewhat strange encounter, I got up in church and went to the front. I said I recently met someone whom I'd known since I was born but she didn't recognise me, but that my Father in heaven would always recognise me. I didn't say it was my mother; I just said "somebody". I don't think anyone twigged.

He's the only Father I believe in now. I will never, ever call the other one 'dad' again. And it's the same with my mother, I suppose.

When I'm at work, every chance I get to mention Jesus, I'll mention his name. They can't believe that this woman they call the Rottweiler has tears in her eyes when I talk about my Lord. And I really do fill up whenever I tell them how I came to Christ on the Away Day.

Anything else, I'm as hard as rock. I used to be one to cry, but not now, unless I think about Jesus. I've stiffened, I've hardened, and I have the ultimate solace, a saving grace. I cry for Jesus and I'd die for Victoria. I get emotional when I see pictures of animal abuse or read about child cruelty in the papers, but otherwise I've accepted that people are people and if something's going to happen, it will. You can't dwell on things.

I pray every day: I pray when I'm driving, I pray when I go to bed; I even pray when I'm Hoovering. If something good happens to me, I thank Him straight away, even if I'm driving the car. And believe me, if you were in the car with me, you'd pray too: I'm not the best behind the wheel and I drive like a bat out of hell.

But I don't just pray when I want something: I pray to thank Him. I thank Him for saving me from Jim, for delivering me from my father, for giving me the guts to see things through when I was down in the gutter. And in truth, for just giving me hope when the world seemed a very hostile and unfriendly place, and true friends were hard to find.

When you can't trust your own parents, you tend to shut yourself off from the outside world and close ranks. Everyone is a potential enemy, rather than a potential friend. You become acutely suspicious of everyone and everything. That's when you need a little help from a higher source.

When your own kith and kin disown you and try to destabilise every facet of your life - in short, become your worst enemy - you have this siege mentality, maybe even paranoia, and it's hard to shake off.

I've got this mother who doesn't even recognise me and when I tell her who I am, she's lukewarm at best and talks to me about her arthritis and dodgy joints. They say absence makes the heart grow fonder – but not in mother's world.

Chapter 17

A Barb from the Grave

Mother died in February 2017, but it would be another year before I found out. She was nothing to me and, just like with my father, her death wasn't bad news; it was just news.

But she couldn't resist a parting shot before she shuffled off. It was a little spike in her will which I'm convinced was meant to torment me from the grave.

She'd left nothing to either Victoria or me, and her will read thus: 'I hereby declare I am making no provision for my daughter, Hazel Valerie Yare, for the reasons set out in a written statement.'

I wasn't in the least bit bothered, nor surprised, that she hadn't left me anything. The surprising thing would have been if she had.

I didn't want any of her money, but I had hoped that she'd leave at least a little bit to Victoria to help with her mortgage. This lovely granddaughter of hers could have paid off some of her mortgage if her grandmother hadn't been such a spiteful old bitch.

But evidently more important to mother was that she got even and left us that final reminder, if one were needed, that we meant nothing to her. I just hope she knew that she meant nothing to me either.

I had to pay a small sum of money to get hold of the will, but I should have known we wouldn't have figured.

"You horrible woman," I thought. "She's trying to leave me in limbo. She's trying to torment me."

I found out she'd left £1,000 to a neighbour and £500 to another couple who lived on her street. I read down the page to see if I could spot Victoria's name anywhere, but to no avail. Not one lousy dime.

Mother had decided to give the remainder to charity. The will said: 'Any money after the property and the estate are sorted, two-thirds go to the Great North Air Ambulance and the other third goes to the British Heart Foundation.'

137

I could well understand why she'd want to leave money to those two charities because my father had received such great care for his heart problems, but I simply can't understand why she made "no provision" for her granddaughter. Was it the falling-out after my dismissal? Quite possibly.

Had it anything to do with the fact that we'd kept Victoria away from her and my father, and for good reason? Most probably.

But I think it largely boils down to her being an evil old woman who couldn't accept that her husband was a womaniser and couldn't forgive me for what she must have perceived to have been the height of betrayal, which was ridiculous, of course, and Victoria was her only granddaughter, for heaven's sake.

She didn't even leave me all the old photos from when I was young. That was mother for you - warped and very vindictive all her life. There was no doubt about it: this was a deliberate, calculated act to get back at me while she still had time. And she obviously wanted to make it as final as possible.

Her death wasn't even in the local newspaper. My parents had always put family deaths in the papers, but I don't think mother wanted people to know she'd passed on because she probably thought I would contest the will.

I found out about her death by accident and immediately started doing some detective work for this book. I rang her number and it was unobtainable. I assumed she was in a nursing home but carried on sleuthing. I presumed she was in the same one that my father had been in, but when I rang them they said there was no-one of that name there.

This woman who answered the phone said: "Try the other one the other side of Yarm. I'll give you the number."

So I rang the other nursing home and this woman said: "Who's calling?"

I said it's someone who used to work with Vi Jackson a long time ago, which was actually true.

"Do you have a Vi Jackson in the nursing home? I enquired.

"Oh, well, we did have," she said. "But I'm afraid she's died."

"Oh, right."

The woman at the care home said mother had died about six months ago, but they got mixed up. I went on the probate site and discovered that she'd actually died in February 2017, some 14 months before I found out. All that time, I thought my mother was still alive but she'd been long gone, though I have no idea how long she'd been in the home.

I didn't even ask what she died of: I presume it was just old age. Nor did I ask where her final resting place was. Just as with my father, I wasn't interested. I imagine it was the crematorium just up the road, but I can't be sure.

She probably thought she'd had the last laugh by leaving me out of the will, but she was wrong because now that she's dead, I can say anything I want about her in this storybook. Nasty, nasty woman, she was, although I still suspect that underneath the steel plate, there was a heart there somewhere.

Me and my mother were by no means opposites, but, somehow, we were antagonists from the start. I'm a bit like her in that I say what I mean, call a spade a spade. Unlike her, I'm a very nice lady, but like her, if anybody crossed me, they wouldn't get a second chance. I will do anything for anybody; I would give them my last penny, but if you cross me I will never see you again.

I just hope that on her death bed she thought about everything and regretted it. You know, I really do believe that in her last hours she had regrets, but only in the sense that she would have felt sorry for herself because she never saw me again and never saw Victoria growing up.

I think back to when I was in America and she was in a right mess. I think back to the gun she kept at the house in case Jim returned, and leaving my nana's sobbing her eyes out after seeing me again after all those years. I just don't get it and I didn't get her. She obviously felt something but could never show it. Why, I don't know. Can't ask her now.

Besides, she hasn't been part of my life for years and now she is history. We're not interested anymore. If we dwell on it, she wins. Jesus teaches you to forgive, but sometimes it's hard, even with a faith as strong as mine. You can forgive people for the way they've treated you or your family, but it doesn't mean that you want them to be a part of your life anymore. In a way, I feel sorry for her because she must have died a lonely death, just like my father.

We are a Christian family in an increasingly unchristian world. Things are getting a bit scary and I don't know how it's all going to turn out. Things could get a whole lot worse for the next generation and they won't have the church to fall back on because hardly anybody goes anymore, certainly not in this country.

I feel sorry for people who haven't got what I have: not just an unshakeable faith, but the greatest friend imaginable who I know will never let me down, my Father in heaven.

Bill, who was one of the biggest sceptics going, is now so immersed in the Christian outlook and the life of the church that he simply can't imagine how he ever lived without it. He goes to the Christian men's breakfasts in Stockton and Middlesbrough and lives and breathes the church.

He went in for an operation recently because his eye had become quite droopy and looked half-closed. He had a cist removed and his bottom eyelid stitched up, to keep the eye in place and make it look less saggy. The operation was a success and he didn't even have to wear a patch. He keeps his old eye in the bedroom as a spare, no doubt to keep an eye on me when he goes out.

Bill has developed another problem in recent years: vascular dementia is slowly eating his memory away. It's still manageable and he can still live a full life; he can see to himself and pluck out historical facts and figures at the drop of a hat. He's a very knowledgeable guy, but his short-term memory is really bad and it drives me mad at times.

I'm so pleased that I still go out to work because it's very hard being with him all day, every day. He forgets people's names and words. His is the least aggressive of the dementias, but I'll say something to him and two minutes later he's forgotten what it was.

Recently, he woke up with blurred vision in his one good eye and I had to take him to hospital. He was unable to read or drive, so they prescribed day and night drops and he's much improved now. Apparently, he had what they call "dry eye" and it made his eye stick closed during the night. He was practically blind when he was at his worst, but he still has his manly duties.

I said to him: "If you go blind, who will put the bins out?"

"You're all heart," he said.

He's 84 now and the years have taken a toll. He has arthritis but he's as fit as a lop in other ways. I still give him his daily chores and he's in good enough shape to take the dogs out. They're not ours: we sometimes look after a Staffy called Chico and a pug named

Tiff: they're our friends' dogs and we love them to bits. Little darlings, they are, and we spoil them rotten. Chico is our neighbours' dog and we looked after him when my neighbour was in hospital. Tiff comes Sunday night to Wednesday teatime. She's the star of the show.

I'm pug crazy. Isn't everyone? So adorable, with their button noses and piggy tails. Our bungalow is like a shrine to them: cute little pug faces adorn my cushions; I have pug ornaments on every shelf and surface, and pug pictures in every room. There are pug and Border Terrier statues in the back yard, where we have a doggy cemetery in memory of those who have left us behind. The ashes of our beloved pets are scattered across the pebbled square which is fenced off and is, to all intents and purposes, a memorial garden.

Of course, I prefer dogs to people, but surely, don't we all? With dogs, it's unconditional love, seven days a week, and who can say that about people? I'd have two or three hundred if I could, or at least ten. They're not like kids - they do as they're told, and they eat what you give them.

We don't have grandkids, but we're ok with that. I'm too busy for grandchildren anyway, even at my age. I'm old enough to be looking back at pictures of my nightmarish past in black-and-white, but I never like to reveal my age. What's the point?

If I retired, I don't know what I'd do with myself. I'm constantly on the go and I'm not really one for tiredness or taking the easy route. When I get home from work, I'll spend three hours writing up reports on my computer, after I've done Bill his tea. It's taken a terrible toll on my back (the work, not Bill's tea), and the pain has been unbearable at times.

I had to use a saddle seat when I was working from home and I went for massages to undo all the knots. I saw a chiropractor for bone treatment. It was she who first mentioned cannabis oil and, at first, I thought she must be joking. But, oh, what a magical thing it was – at first. It's great for aches and paints and the joints, if you'll excuse the pun.

Thanks to a change in the law, I could buy it over the counter and it got rid of the pain straight away. The cannabis comes in sunflower oil and they had a buy-one, get-one free offer, so I was buying two at a time, positively gorging on the stuff.

To all intents and purposes, I was a cannabis junky, but on a purely medicinal level. It was like a miracle cure and I had the benefit of what felt like a completely new back. What's more, I was sleeping like a baby and eating better than ever. But then it started to have a very bad effect on me. I became ill and couldn't work. I think it was a build-up of the stuff which had got into my system over time. I was doubled up with pain in my stomach and I was very sick. I suppose it doesn't suit everyone – shame.

But I'm still going out to work because I genuinely love the job that I do. Some are genuinely in wonder at how I manage to continue working in such a demanding and stressful environment, post-retirement age. All my work has come from recommendations and I still have regular customers who I see either weekly, monthly, quarterly or annually.

"You'll be coming in here until you're 90, on your zimmer frame!" they'll say.

People find it hard to believe that I stay relatively young-looking for someone who was conceived when the bombs were dropping on Middlesbrough. They can't believe it when I tell them my true age.

"It the injections!" I tell them.

They just laugh.

Considering what I've been though, I should be haggard like a wizened old spinster, but I'm just the opposite. I have no grey hairs and I am what polite society might call a superannuated strawberry blonde. I lost my red hair literally overnight when Bill had his heart attack in 2004. It must have been the shock, I guess.

"I knew I'd get the blame!" Bill said at the time.

I'll tell you my secret and it's nothing fancy: anti-wrinkle fillers. I still go in for the odd injection, but it's not botox – that's poison. The fillers contain hyaluronic acid: it's something we have in us naturally, but it gets less as we get older. It holds a thousand times itself in water and plumps out the skin. The injections last about two years.

I'm still fit and strong and sharp of mind, and still very passionate about health and safety. Somebody at work once said I was like a Yorkshire Terrier: "Once she gets her teeth into something, she never lets go."

Well, yes, and I'll take that as a compliment. I'm only 5ft but I'd take on King Kong if you got me a pair of stilts. When I snap, I imagine I'm not a pretty sight. I lose my rag with Bill when he forgets things, but he can't help it 'cos he's got dementia.

I'm the one they could never tire out. I've been in this line of work for nearly 30 years and people now say: "Oh, is she still there? She frightens the life out of me!"

Jim's still out there as far as I know: Seventy-nine years old and still looking deeply suspect, going on the few pictures I've seen on the internet.

I trawled the web and found his address in a city in east Texas, and I must say his house looked surprisingly nice. The land registry says he bought the house in 2015 with a five-year mortgage, so it can't have been worth much, but it's surrounded by much bigger houses and it looks a very nice area. I can't imagine how he got the money to live in a place like that 'cos I found out that he'd been declared bankrupt twice - in 2008 and 2012 - although he was eventually discharged. He also had a few DUIs to his name (that's American slang for driving under the influence, if you didn't already know). But Jim always gets off the hook.

I went on this other website which gives criminal and prison records in return for a subscription fee. It turns out that Jim was in prison when he was 47, but it didn't say what for. Funnily enough, years ago - I think it was in the mid-80s - Bill and I were watching a programme about US penitentiaries and I could have sworn I saw Jim in there, wearing an orange jumpsuit.

I said to Bill: "Bloody hell, I could swear that was Jim!"

His last wife, Charlene - whom Jim married in 1968, two years after I fled the States - died in August 2006, aged 64, just five months after they got divorced. I can only imagine the poor woman suffered terribly, but she stayed with him for 40 years, so perhaps the marriage was a happy one, or maybe she just had the patience of a saint. Or perhaps she actually left him years before then.

Strangely, she was registered at two different addresses in Gregg County, Texas, plus another one in Mansfield, Louisiana - Jim's old stomping ground.

The birth, marriage and death records show that he wedded a Carol Elizabeth, aged 20, on December 29, 1964, just 15 months before he married me. The wedding was in Shelby, Texas, where

Jim appears to have rounded off the Christmas festivities with a shotgun wedding.

But those are just two of the marriages recorded on this one website. I think it's undeniable that there were many others – his own mother told me that.

There are other records I've found online which appear to back up Fanny's revelations all those years ago. There are also incidents of a domestic nature (presumably violence) logged against his name. The records also confirm he had lots of children to different women. Surprisingly, one of the children was adopted.

According to my calculations, he's had seven wives including me.

For all I know, he could be on Number 8 by now. I wouldn't put it past him to have shacked up with another woman, even approaching his 80s. Despite all I've said about him, he's definitely got something, and he was an exceptional lover. It would be easy for a woman to fall for his lies.

The internet has opened up a whole new world to me and I've immersed myself in it completely. I'm on Facebook and I've got WhatsApp; I'm a woman of the modern age and I daily post pictures of cute pug puppies doing funny things and regularly upload animal-welfare videos and petitions. But I also keep an eye out for Jim 'cos you're bound to be curious after 50 years of merciful separation.

To be honest, I thought someone would have shot him by now, but evidently not. He might be a reformed character, who knows?

All his siblings are dead: Willis Oneal, Charlie Rogers, Alice Fay, Aubrey. All gone, but Jim still looms large.

His mother died in November 1973, aged 72. Charlie Rogers went nine years later, quickly followed by Willis Oneal. Both brothers died in Texas.

His sister Alice Faye passed away in 1998, aged 60. His third brother, Aubrey, died in Harris County, Texas, in August 1999, aged 67.

Jim's the only one left, which doesn't seem entirely fair. I don't understand why the no-good waster won't die. After all, he must have a liver like an old kettle. The devil looks after his own, I suppose. I honestly can't understand how he's not been murdered.

I was speaking to my friend Dorothy recently and I told her about what happened to me all those years ago. She couldn't believe I'd never told her before.

I've known her for over 30 years and I'd never breathed a word, then I told her I had a book coming out.

"Why did you marry him if he had five wives?" she asked, incredulous.

I told her I had no idea he was a polygamist and that he had no divorces, and that as far as the state was concerned, his marital record was unblemished.

"No!" she said.

Just recently, I saw a picture of him buying a car at a garage in Texas, wearing a cap and shaking this guy's hand. I wouldn't have recognised him in the street – he looked even older than Bill. But at length I realised it was unmistakably him: rakish and stick thin. He looked proper white-trash hillbilly, Texan-style.

I keep Jim in the back of my mind – but well to the back. My estranged daughter Hazel is near the back too, but she is never forgotten. When I picture her in her swaddling clothes, that beaming little smile and twinkling eyes, it makes me smile. When I recall that Hazel is a by-product of Jim, my brow furrows.

The only time I think of her is on her birthday. I will not disclose what that is to protect her identity: for all I know, she might be reading this. I just hope she is happy and has a good life.

Bill and I were watching a TV programme about adoption one day and it gave you a number to ring the Adoption Society if you were looking to get in touch with a long-lost son or daughter. I said to Bill that I didn't want to get in touch with Hazel, but if she wanted to ring me, that was fine.

Usually, adopted children start getting curious about their biological parents when they're about 18. After that, they start to lose interest.

Hazel will be in her early 50s now and must surely have lost interest in me. At least, she's never been in touch, and neither have I.

I'm not her mother; I only gave birth to her. I haven't gone through life with her, the ups and downs of adolescence and early adulthood. Presumably - hopefully - her adoptive parents did all that.

I do not know how I'd react if I saw her again. It could be a disaster on a par with my encounter with mother at the Marton Hotel & Country Club, or it might rekindle a magical new friendship. But it's all academic, because it will never happen.

I have absolutely no doubt that if I had kept Hazel, Bill would have treated her as one of his own. But then I wouldn't have had any more children, and therefore we'd never have had Victoria, which is unthinkable. Things always work out for a reason, that's how I look at it. It's all in God's plan.

Bill's always been a softy and Victoria's just like him. I don't give people a second chance if they've done me wrong, but Victoria will say: "Oh, give 'em a second chance, mam."

She still has ME - it doesn't just go away - but it hasn't surfaced for a long time. When it does, she just has to sleep.

She still works for the Department for Work and Pensions at the Jobcentre in Middlesbrough after a spell with the Student Loans company in Darlington, a PPI firm called Fast Track and Virgin Media. Money can be a struggle for her at times and her mortgage is still not paid off.

I know I'm her mother, but I say in all honesty that she is one of the kindest people I know. She's good with everyone; just an amazing person. Everyone is the same in her eyes.

She's very popular at work and a goddess to the needy. We've had drug addicts and alcoholics come to the ministries and she's always one of the first to welcome them in. They are given a bacon sandwich and a cup of coffee, somewhere to get out of the cold. Admittedly, some do turn up to steal, but most just want some company and a bite to eat.

The church saves lives and if you don't believe me, then ask Gram Seed, whose story is nothing short of a modern miracle.

Gram, who now heads his own church ministry called Sowing Seeds, was a juvenile delinquent and went on to become a drug addict, alcoholic, shoplifter, counterfeiter and Middlesbrough football hooligan. He used to sell fake clothes and was in and out of prison for years.

He was notorious, and not just in Middlesbrough. He used to travel down to places like Millwall with the Middlesbrough hooligan crew but not to watch the matches – he went to fight. He was stabbed multiple times and suffered many serious beatings during

146

a long criminal career. He did several stretches behind bars and ended up as a tramp, sleeping on the same bench in the centre of Middlesbrough for three-and-a-half years, barely eating and with no control over his bodily functions. He used to sit in his own urine and faeces.

Gram's situation was about as desperate as it could get: his family and the police thought he was a lost cause and it was only a matter of time before his battered body gave up. Somebody once took a hammer to his head, then he was knifed and lost a finger. He even lost his sight for a while and had these big scars all over his body. He was 6ft 6in but his body had been ravaged, seemingly beyond repair.

People would go to the bench to feed him from time to time, but it looked like he was on the way out. A group of Christians, who walked the streets to help the sick and needy, went to see him and said: "Jesus loves you."

"Why would Jesus love a scumbag like me?" said Gram.

Those same Christians wouldn't give up, even when all seemed lost. One day, he collapsed in the street and was rushed into James Cook Hospital. He fell into a six-day coma and the doctors had all but given up on him. He was only 32.

They found his mother and told her they couldn't do anything for him. He was full of tubes and wires and they said the best thing would be to turn off the life-support machine. But she said: "No, he's only 32."

But those same Christians who had gone to see him on the bench found out where he was and asked his mother if they could pray for him.

"Well, you might as well," she said. "There's nothing else gonna save him."

So they went into the hospital and prayed and prayed and prayed. And unbelievably, he came out of the coma. And he's never touched a drink, smoked or taken any drugs since. He found God in hospital – the very same one where my Victoria found salvation.

All he's done since is tell people about Jesus and how He saved his life. He goes into prisons, schools and young-offenders' institutions, and tells people about his own experiences, how he was saved by his new faith, and about what can happen to them if they don't change their ways.

It's a remarkable story of hope and redemption, and of course the power and miracles of God, and true faith as a great healer.

Gram now runs Sowing Seeds Ministries, a Christian charity in Stockton-on-Tees which brings the message and love of Christ to young prisoners, ex-offenders, drug users, alcoholics, or people who have just lost their way in life. He also runs an Alpha course for people who want to know about Christianity.

If Gram can make it, anyone can. Indeed, you could say the same about me, though we were from completely different walks of life. I got to know him through my daughter who used to go to his ministry. He told me that when he came out of the coma, he felt like he was being bathed in pure water.

It's clear to me now that what happened to Gram was a miracle. He said he was in one prison and at the end of his talk, he said if anyone wanted to give their life to Jesus, please stand up. All 19 prisoners got to their feet - the prison wardens too. That is very powerful.

Gram is now married with two boys. One of them is a brilliant footballer who's on Hartlepool's books and the older lad's a wrestler. Gram's was a life saved, and now he's saving lives.

We once had someone who came to the ministry who said he was about to take his own life. He had these tablets and went for a walk beside the river in Stockton to overdose on them, but he passed the Sowing Seeds centre on the way and saw the cross lit up in the window. And he thought: "Oh, I wonder what's in there?"

He opened the door to have a look inside and that was it: he threw the tablets away the very next day. Another one saved.

Gram's house is still raided by police because they still think he's up to something, but nothing could be further from the truth. They should just leave him alone because he's done nothing wrong and is a man of God now. People are jealous, you see, and tip police off about him. A leopard *can* change its spots, but people are so sceptical they don't want to believe it.

When police turn up to search his house, Gram says: "Go on then. Jesus loves you, ya know."

148

One of these policemen was the last one to put Gram in prison, but Gram has since baptised him, so now they're good friends. Gram's 52 now – 20 years sober.

Our church, Jubilee, is flourishing and the numbers are getting bigger, as are evangelical churches everywhere. Elsewhere, the picture is grim: the Anglican Church is in an awful mess, congregations are dwindling, but they've only got themselves to blame. Their services are boring; they're staid and conventional. You're never going to attract the young ones if all you do is sit down on pews and pray. At our church, we sing and dance and even do a Conga line from time to time. We fly flags of all the countries; we have international days; we are inclusive.

The Church of England needn't moan about people not coming through the doors and they should stop harping on about the moral vacuum, though of course we're staring at a crisis of epic proportions. For goodness' sake, they don't even have morning assembly at school anymore, except at Catholic schools. And the Catholic church should get off its moral high horse and stop being so political.

Nowadays, you'd be hard pressed to find more than two or three people at worship in your average Anglican church – and that includes the organist. We have about two or three hundred every week. Our church is from all nations and backgrounds, but God sees us all the same. We're all His children.

If you walked into our church on a Sunday, you'd be amazed by the atmosphere which is just electric and everybody would be kissing and cuddling you. We have a charity called Open Door that helps asylum seekers and refugees. We have houses for them to live in and we help them with English and many other things.

Eighteen years now I've been a Christian. Newspapers talk about the demise of Christianity, but the Evangelical church is just getting bigger. There's a massive revival.

There's a church in central London that takes a cathedral over every weekend and needs two services on a Sunday to fit everyone in. That's two different congregations and I don't know how many thousands of people at each service. These things are going on all the time but are never reported in the newspapers. They're only interested when they hear about some salacious gossip or the latest sexual transgression by some disgraced priest.

149

Sylvester Stallone became a Christian and barely anyone heard about it. But if the media said he was gay, which he most clearly isn't, it would be all over the papers.

An Anglican daughter of one of Bill's friends goes to a local church where there's barely a bum on a pew. She once went to an evening service and there was just her, the choir and the organist. The choir were so embarrassed for her, they said: "Come and sit with us."

This void, the demise of the traditional, antiquated church, has been filled by immorality, drugs and material things. Look at all the big shopping centres – they're built like cathedrals, but even they're on the slide. Now we have the internet, which means there's no real need for commercial buildings. It's getting a bit scary. I don't think anyone really likes how it's all turned out.

Maybe we should rip it all up and start again, just like I did.

Afterword

Memories of America and the Deep South burn deep into my brain to this day. I've looked at pictures of Mansfield on Google Earth and it has changed beyond recognition. The shacks have all gone, replaced by posh houses, restaurants and hotels.

For some reason, it made me quite upset. The streets are lined with trees, bushes and privet hedges, and the place looks immaculate, but it's lost that old-world charm.

Seventy-seven per cent of the population is now African-American. When I was there in the 60s, the ratio was the other way around: 70:30 in the whites' favour, which is probably why Jim moved to Texas.

I guess he fled Louisiana during the "white flight" back to the Lone Star State, where he'd be with people of his own ilk. Jim was never going to be at home with racial integration - it's anathema to him.

I went the other way, embracing as many different cultures and ethnicities as I could. We have people from all over the world at our church. We pray for them and each other, and we pray for those who have died. We have a large immigrant community in Middlesbrough and at Jubilee Church we welcome them all with open arms.

Two of our best friends are a lovely Iranian couple called Mahvash and Soroush, who have become cherished members of the church community.

Soroush, who is now an Elder in the church, fled Iran after being tortured for being a Christian. Over there, Christianity is still an underground movement, a pariah faith, and the Christians are persecuted something terrible. They're not even allowed to sing at worship.

Soroush - his and Mahvash's families are both Muslims - was captured and tortured twice, and all because he went to a Christian church that was forcedly clandestine. In Iran, you can't have a passport unless you've done National Service, but Soroush's father managed to get him one. My friend had to get through a whole load

151

of checkpoints and random vehicle stops to get out of the country, knowing that if they caught him again, that would be the last his family saw of him. Mahvash, his wife, went with him and by some miracle, they managed to dodge the checks and made it over to the UK.

People like Mahvash and Saroush are living perfectly respectable, blameless lives and can only enrich this country of ours. They are wonderful hosts and sometimes invite me and Bill over for dinner. The food is out of this world.

We have been to the homes of several Iranian families for meals. They are all wonderful cooks and their hospitality is second to none. The problem is that certain sections of the media tend to concentrate on the negative side of our new, multicultural age.

Of course, it would be silly and disingenuous to overlook the problem we have with sex trafficking and forced prostitution. There has been a massive number of police raids in Middlesbrough, particularly around Longford Street, where they found kidnapped girls being used as sex slaves in these houses rented by pimps.

There was a Nigerian girl who went to our church who had been kidnapped back in her homeland and used as a sex slave. She was such a nice girl: it's tragic that these things happen in the 21st century.

There's this stigma about immigration and there's this belief, fuelled by the press, that most people who come here from a foreign country are here to rob and steal and sponge off the state. In my experience, nothing could be further from the truth.

There are always going to be a few bad apples and tensions in certain communities, but if you came to our church on a Sunday, you would find a happy, harmonious melting pot of all the nationalities, all mingled together under the banner of Christ. There are no nationalities, no divisions, as far as we are concerned. We are one big, happy family.

Sadly, we've lost some of our international friends along the way: some have had to move on; others have been caught up in Government red tape or fallen foul of the asylum system for one reason or other. One of our Afghan boys, a lovely lad in his late 20s who had converted to Christianity and was much-loved in our community, was sent back home because he was an unprocessed

rest all the bad memories and enjoy the good times in the twilight of my life.

I am proud of the woman I am today because I went through a hell of a time becoming her, but without Jesus I wouldn't be that woman: a wife, a mother and now an adoptive grandmother to three beautiful children.

I thank God, and Him alone, for carrying me through all the hard times and never leaving me. Amen.

Also written by Nick Towle

The Forgotten Champ: John L Gardner

He was the Hackney Rock, the 'Mini Marciano', king of the British and European heavyweights, yet somewhere down the line John L Gardner became the 'Forgotten Champ'.

Terrorised by a brutal father, shunned by his peers, his was a torrid childhood in the deprived East End where his only friends were his doting mother and an Alsatian called Vic.

But a chance encounter with Dr Who and the wiles of his gangster brother led Gardner to the attention of unscrupulous boxing moguls who turned him into an irresistible force but took his spoils in the process.

At his peak, Gardner was nigh-on unbeatable. He faced down the gruesome Paul Sykes, went toe-to-toe with Ali and had a strange encounter with Freddie Starr and a UFO.

He fought the law, battled a rampant gambling habit and ultimately stared down his most resilient foe - the 'Big C'.

In this absorbing and unflinching account of his stellar career, Gardner lifts the lid on how he was betrayed by some of the biggest names in boxing. How he conquered half the world but preferred to shun the limelight.

Moving, funny and at times tragic, his remarkable story is a must-read for all fans of the noble art.

With Nick Towle

ISBN: 978-0-9955312-9-1

Also written by Nick Towle

Blood is Only Red Sweat
Dave 'The Beast' Radford

The blood-spattered world of bare-knuckle boxing is the ultimate test for the fist merchants of the modern era, and they come no more fearsome than the man they call The Beast.

The mere mention of the name Dave Radford is enough to send shivers down the spines of even the most hardened bare-knuckle warriors.

The Yorkshire lion heart roared into the UK knuckle pit after a terrible accident down a shaft spelled the end of what promised to be a glittering professional career with the gloves. Not to be deterred, The Beast simply whipped the gloves off and unleashed his own brand of hell on the unforgiving world of knuckle boxing.

Here, in his own words, the man who shot to the stars then crashed back down to earth tells it like it is in a brutally-candid account of his rollercoaster journey back to the Elysian Fields of the noble art...

'To the Lions, Blood is Nectar' Mark Kram.